The Revd Dr Ali Green fir[ ] [ ]
before becoming co-found[ ] [ ]-
sultancy. She has spent [ ] n
England and Wales, as a lay lea[ ] ly,
as a priest. She worked for several years a[ ] nd
lecturer in a men's prison, and is currently a priest in the
diocese of Monmouth. She is the Wales representative for
the Ecumenical Forum of European Christian Women, and
is the author of *A Theology of Women's Priesthood* (SPCK,
2009).

A PRIESTHOOD OF BOTH SEXES

Paying attention to difference

ALI GREEN

First published in Great Britain in 2011

Society for Promoting Christian Knowledge
36 Causton Street
London SW1P 4ST
www.spckpublishing.co.uk

British Library Cataloguing-in-Publication Data
A catalogue record for this book is available from the British Library

ISBN 978–0–281–06353–6

1 3 5 7 9 10 8 6 4 2

Typeset by Graphicraft Ltd, Hong Kong
Printed in Great Britain by Ashford Colour Press

Produced on paper from sustainable forests

Contents

Acknowledgements

I owe an enormous debt of gratitude to my many brothers and sisters in Christ across the globe who got to hear about my project and responded by meeting with me personally or corresponding by phone and email. Without their sharing very personal stories and heartfelt experiences, this book would not have emerged. In most cases, I have changed names throughout the book in order to preserve their privacy.

1

Introduction

Paying attention to difference

On a cold February day in 1966, in a New York studio, soul singer James Brown recorded a song that would become a best seller, one of the staples of his live shows. Nearly forty years later it was ranked number 123 by the magazine *Rolling Stone* in its list of the five hundred greatest songs of all times. The same magazine described the lyrics as 'almost biblically chauvinistic'. Ironically, perhaps, they were co-written by a woman, Betty Newsome:

> This is a man's world, this is a man's world
> But it wouldn't be nothing, nothing without a woman or
> a girl.

It remains a truism, nearly half a century after that song was first written, that we live in a man's world. We mostly take it for granted, wherever we live, in whatever culture, that male ways of thinking, speaking and behaving are the norm – something that from now on I will call a male taken-for-grantedness, or T-for-G. Whenever it is assumed that there is just one way of organizing a structure or carrying out a process, or even of changing that culture, then it is likely to be according to patterns of male T-for-G.

In my book *A Theology of Women's Priesthood*, I aimed to take sexual difference seriously as a fundamental principle in understanding the nature of reality. It is a vital thread that runs through the warp and weft of all our being and doing. Women's experience of religion, as with all human life, is different from that of men, and this difference relates to how the sexes are differently positioned in culture. The Church, male-dominated throughout its history, has largely left women without a place or a voice, leaving them eavesdroppers on Scripture, language and ritual, and excluded from leadership. So in religion, as in other aspects of life, women struggle to achieve full identity and personhood. Women themselves, because they are embedded in male T-for-G, are not necessarily aware that there are other, equally valid ways of knowing and behaving apart from male ones that we take for granted as normative for all society, for women as well as men. Even when women are consciously seeking alternatives, it is still difficult to forge a transition from old, established ways. This is true in every sector of society, including the Church (by which I mean the whole Christian family, the body of Christ, rather than a particular denomination).

I suggested in *A Theology of Women's Priesthood* that where women and men minister together as priests, there is the potential for the Church to grow towards a new way of being, one that is closer to the Kingdom of God because it offers a model of the body of Christ which honours all its members in their discipleship and ministry. A priesthood of both sexes, I reasoned, affirms that the female as well as the male body mediates the divine. I focused on the symbol and narrative of the Christian religion, particularly as they appear in the language and ritual of the Eucharist. I argued that a woman priest, because she carries symbols associated with the female body, enriches the range and depth of symbolic meanings that have been restricted in the formation of thought, language and culture. A priesthood of two equal sexes represents not a minor adjustment in the status quo but the herald of a new way of being Church. A priesthood of women and men in partnership affirms the value – in fact the necessity – of male and female working together to help redeem a broken world. It offers hope that, freed from male-dominated ways of hearing, understanding and responding to its faith story, the Church will help all people, female and male, to reach their full potential as children of God.

Having made the case for recognizing and honouring sexual difference, I concluded by expressing my hope for a 'harmonious, fruitful and mutually respectful partnership' between the sexes, in a Church that celebrates the 'God-given male–female bond' in its ministry (2009:170). Thus I offered a vision of a priesthood of both sexes that would bring us closer to a Kingdom-shaped Church and set an example for society. What I want to do in *A Priesthood of Both Sexes* is to answer the question: how does a theology built on sexual difference manifest itself in the life and ministry of practising priests and in the lives of those to whom they minister? The challenge I have set myself here is of finding and reflecting on examples of such a theology in real situations.

Some key terms

Before explaining how I have gone about finding answers to my question, I give below a brief explanation of some key terms and concepts that will crop up in the following chapters. These are all important in the context of my theology of a priesthood of both sexes, and they also have a bearing on what the life and ministry of such a priesthood might look like in practice.

Symbol

A symbol stands for something – or usually a range of things – other than itself. It starts with something we know and reaches out towards what is difficult to understand or describe. Water, for instance, can act as a symbol of new life, as in baptism. It can signify refreshment and well-being, as in the still waters of Psalm 23. It can also stand for chaos, death or malevolence – as in the opening of Psalm 69:

> Save me, O God,
> for the waters have come up to my neck.
> I sink in deep mire,
> where there is no foothold;
> I have come into deep water,
> and the floods sweep over me.

Symbols are essential to the way we understand ourselves and the way we think. Because they can take us from our everyday world into the realm of the sacred, they are essential to our religious experience. The symbolic language of religion – in Scripture, in ritual and worship – acts as a window on transcendent realities that are otherwise beyond the limitations of rational thought. Bread, for instance, is a staple item of food that many of us eat daily. In the context of worship, however, it brings to mind a range of qualities that reach far beyond the concrete reality of a humble loaf. The bread broken at the Eucharist stands for the broken Body of Christ, and for ourselves as Christ's Body the Church. It also points towards our calling to feed and care for a broken world, and to live in loving fellowship with one another and with creation. Our religious language and experience is heightened by such symbols. Their powerful resonance requires us to respond – in the case of the shared bread of the Eucharist, by recommitting ourselves (according to the words of the eucharistic liturgy) to go in peace to love and serve the Lord.

For symbols to remain active and potent, they have to be experienced as valid. Some symbols – or particular meanings attached to them – may become archaic or invalid or sometimes even repulsive over a period of time. The word 'horn' occurs in many Old Testament books to signify the Lord's anointed one or the strength and vigour of the people of God. For modern readers, however, much of its original significance has been lost. So we have to work harder at gaining the meaning behind the image. Many of our ancient religious symbols require reinterpretation so that they continue to speak to us powerfully. When they do this effectively, they help us to find our own identity, to become aware of the sacred, and to articulate and respond to transcendent realities.

This is true of the priesthood, which carries a great raft of meanings that point to the sacred and to our understanding of ourselves as creatures of God. In the past few years the traditional symbolism associated with priesthood in the Anglican Church has undergone a shift. Until very recently, priesthood was an exclusively male preserve, which reflected male ways of knowing, language and behaviour. The ordination of women has caused something of a collision of time-honoured symbolic associations that obliges us to think again about our understanding of God, of ourselves and our relationship with others. It makes us reconsider our God-talk – the language of worship and liturgy, our interpretation of Scripture – and the way we live in the world.

To take an example: symbols around birthing, nurturing, caring and flourishing apply most readily to women. This is not to say that a woman has to be a mother in order for these symbols to work. As humans we have all been born of a woman, so these symbolic connections are accessible to everyone while being more obviously carried by women. Metaphors of female bodiliness are most often linked with nature, sexuality, motherhood and birth. We talk, for example, of 'mother earth' as the planet which supports us, and 'mother nature' for the natural environment that nourishes us; and we symbolically link nurturing care with the maternal body by speaking of 'the milk of human kindness'.

Christian Scripture and tradition have offered a dualistic view of womanhood, women's bodies and the feminine: a black-and-white contrast between the unique, virginal, asexual, saintly figure of Mary and the sinful Eve and her descendants, whose sexuality and sensuality are linked with impurity and adultery. There has been a paucity of images modelling femininity and metaphors that uphold women's experience and the real, sensuous female body as a focus for encountering the sacred. However, in the woman priest we now have such a focus. Here is someone who represents both God and the Church, both the feminine in God who is neither male nor female, the maternal Creator whom we come to know and love by being born again; and real women, whose bodies and ways of knowing are different from those of men.

Sexual difference

Difference is fundamental to human experience. Women and men differ in terms of physiological function, inherited characteristics and cultural influences. The way that women and men experience the world differs in a way that reaches beyond

5

biological sex and gender. But a culture of male T-for-G ignores sexual difference. This male bias is generally the result not of a conscious decision to exclude women, but rather an assumption that the male is normative and so stands for humanity. Leonardo da Vinci produced a sketch of an outstretched naked male figure, known as 'Vitruvian Man'. It is usually described in terms of a model of the ideal of humanity, showing the proportions of the human figure. Actually, what it shows is an explicitly male figure. The female body has its own distinct shape with different proportions. But thanks to male T-for-G, da Vinci's sketch is unapologetically described as fully representative of all human beings. How might we react if we were told we were about to see an idealized figure of a human being, and then were shown a sketch of a naked woman? Barely anyone would expect to see a female representing all of humanity, even if the viewer were herself female.

In a culture of male T-for-G, thought and language spring from the male imagination while overlooking or undervaluing the female. Where identity, logic and rationality are symbolically male, man is taken as central and normative, while woman is the 'other', the binary opposite. Women are seen to be less in the image of God and inferior and subordinate to men, even less than fully human. There is an assumption across organizations that their cultures are ungendered, whereas they actually originate and operate from a masculine imagination and worldview. In the Church, an all-male hierarchy perpetuated such a gendered culture with its own masculine ways of knowing, of language and of behaviour, and these both reflected and influenced the symbolic meanings associated with priesthood.

Where there exists a priesthood of both men and women, then there is bound to be something of a collision of cultures because sexual difference has been introduced into an exclusively male preserve. The presence of women priests requires the Church to look seriously at the principle of sexual difference. It means addressing traditional ways of thinking and acting that have left women as 'others', without a voice or a place. Many symbolic meanings in our religious language and practice either ignore or undervalue or even demean women and the feminine. There is still a vast gap between women's experience and the culture of the Church; but where there is a priesthood of both men and women, the closing of that gap can begin. A church that acknowledges and upholds models both of femininity and masculinity, and values women's as well as men's experience and ways of knowing, can free itself from its historically male-dominated ways of hearing, understanding and responding to the Christian story.

One of the tasks necessary along this path is to tackle some of the negative symbolic meanings associated with women. The woman priest has begun this journey – the simple fact of women's priesthood itself challenges some of the negative symbolism which has burdened women hitherto. Hence religious symbols can be renewed, enriched and transformed so as to help everyone, including women and others historically on the outside, to flourish and to reach their full potential as children of God. In other words, a priesthood of both sexes, aware of its potential to transform and revitalize ancient symbolic meanings, can help us towards being the inclusive, welcoming community that Jesus modelled in his ministry.

Women's experience and way of knowing

Researchers, whether anthropologists or psychologists, sociologists or theologians, have begun to realize that women's ways of being and doing are different from those of men and that a fuller understanding of people and communities is incomplete as long as half the human race is overlooked. Research in any field must pay heed to the voices of women themselves, however muted they are in a culture of male T-for-G. But it is difficult to imagine what a female culture, or a culture of two equal genders, might look like. As Sheila Durkin Dierks observes, 'It has been happening for thousands of years. Men decide what women are and then tell us' (1997:22). We have no way of knowing how we would encode knowledge or express desire or symbolize the sacred or do anything else within an alternative order. We have no record of such a world,

7

and so we cannot tell how male and female experience would manifest itself there.

The language and behaviour of male T-for-G reflects and reinforces men's world-view and leaves women deprived of a language and desire that is appropriate to them. In religious institutions, as elsewhere, it has restricted the potential and aspirations of women, suppressing their own way of knowing and pressuring them to imitate male ways rather than to bring their own particular experience, wisdom and gifts.

Women's experience and voice were rare among the annals of theology until feminist theology began, albeit without many of the usual historical benchmarks and structures that support the long-standing traditions of academic discourse. Feminist theologians have uncovered many themes and stories that have been overlooked, because theology thus far was largely done by men, with the result that women's presence and women's voices have been lost or neglected. Feminist theology, challenging the ascendancy of the male, asserts that women are made equally with men in God's image, and that women's experience is as valid and as valuable as that of men.

Inclusivity

The gospel message of Jesus was one of radical inclusivity. Jesus welcomed lepers, Roman soldiers, prostitutes, rich tax collectors and poor widows alike. His community of followers was made up of men and women from many walks of life: no one had to pass a test of fitness to be allowed in. From the earliest generations of Christians, baptism was open to women and men, boys and girls, master and slave, Jew and Gentile. It took over as the distinguishing imprint of belief from the Jewish all-male practice of circumcision. Baptism signalled that redemption and the gifts of the Spirit were available to all people without distinction.

Today we are still working out what that principle of inclusivity means. Each generation uncovers another lingering layer of excluding alienation – slavery, class structures, sexism – which has to be overcome in order for the Church to be true to its calling as the body of Christ. If we see our Christian ministry as offering a message of liberation and hope to all people, then we have to make sure that the message is inclusive for all people. If we take seriously Jesus' teaching that the good news is for everyone, then we must continue to root out any traditions and practices that exclude people for no just cause. We will want to make our liturgy, our God-talk, our pastoral ministry and every aspect of church life as inclusive as possible, because this is the example that our Master has given us in his ministry and teaching.

The challenge

Having set myself the challenge of finding examples of a priesthood that honours sexual difference in its practical theology, I looked at places of ministry where both male and female priests operate together. So some parishes and situations, where there are priests of only one sex, had to be eliminated from my search. I drew up a list of features which, in terms of the theology that I had developed, I would expect to be present where sexual difference is taken seriously as a fundamental principle. In other words, these would be places where male T-for-G is recognized and addressed, where the female voice is given expression, and where models of femininity are equally valued with masculine ones. These issues would be regarded as important for several reasons, as I will explain more fully in the following pages. But very briefly, they bear upon our understanding of the nature of God; they help both men and women to flourish as children of God; and they influence the way we act in the wider world.

I did not set out in hope of finding the Holy Grail. There does not exist, I concluded in my previous book, a real community whose members conform to all the ideals in relationship either with God or with one another, according to the criteria I had set out. In fact, with a degree of scepticism based on my previous experience and research, I assumed that it would have been far easier to compile a book of lamentations on what goes

9

wrong, and a catalogue of where we fall short in the matter of sexual difference. The priesthood, as with every community since the fall of Adam and Eve, is riven with difficulties stemming from the brokenness between the sexes, and tales of hurt, frustration and disillusion are only too easy to find. What I was hoping to find, however, were oases of hope and harmony that tell the *good* news – places and situations where women and men are operating side by side in productive, mutually respectful and supportive ministry, celebrating rather than ignoring sexual difference, and setting a model for others to follow.

I have limited my search almost exclusively to the Anglican Church, because that is both my own place of ministry and also the subject of my previous book. The matter of women's priesthood is still very much a live issue in the Anglican Communion. By the beginning of this century, a slim majority of Anglican provinces were ordaining women as deacons and priests. Furthermore, the Province of Aotearoa, New Zealand and Polynesia, as well as Canada and the USA, had female bishops. But some provinces that ordain women priests do not accept female bishops. And in provinces where women are priests some dioceses and parishes still do not accept their priesthood. So it is timely now, for those who do recognize a priesthood of both sexes, to reflect on sexual difference in the priesthood and its effect on practical ministry. Since the Anglican Church is global, I have gathered stories and comments from across the world, from Wales to New Zealand, Hong Kong to Uganda.

Areas of inquiry

In all the places and situations I studied, I covered four broad areas of inquiry, each of which I report and reflect on in the following chapters.

The first area relates sexual difference to personal identity. We each have a sense of self that develops according to the environment and culture in which we exist, and which helps (or hinders) our maturing to full personhood. For Christians, that personal identity is grounded in our self-understanding as creatures of God. The priest's sense of self is moulded not only by this understanding but also by the symbolic meanings associated with the priestly vocation. He or she represents the Godhead to the Church and to the whole community, and represents them before the Godhead. Priests offer an array of metaphors relating to the divine, to the Church and to all of creation. These symbolic meanings are often themselves gendered, varying according to the sex of the one carrying any given symbolism.

A priest's sense of identity develops during a long process of formation through discernment, selection, training and ministry. During all that time, the extent to which priests are aware of their own distinct, gendered symbolic resonance, and the way they interpret that resonance, influences both their personal self-image and the way they model ministry and discipleship.

Second, a recognition of sexual difference affects our God-talk. A great deal of the language and ritual of religion is gendered, so that there is a distinct symbolism associated with each sex. It is also usually the case in religious language that the male is associated more closely with God and with humanity, while the female is associated with nature and the body, earthliness and proneness to sin. God has been imagined by and large in the male image. An exclusively male priesthood perpetuated this image, implying that maleness was more closely associated with divinity, and only men could represent Christ for the priesthood of the whole Church.

Women were left with only masculine concepts of subjectivity and masculine God-talk. The feminine insight into the divine was ignored or suppressed and sometimes reviled. Girls were taught that they were inferior as a sex and more prone to sin. Women, as the 'other' in the masculine mind, personified the physical – reproductive function, sexual attraction, emotions, things earthly and close to nature. Men, by contrast, personified the spiritual, the rational, the intellectual. From this perspective, women's bodies – and women in general – were quite dangerous and required oversight by men. Priests who take sexual difference seriously will be aware of the genderedness of these symbolic associations and will seek to uphold the feminine as a valid focus for the divine, in prayer, teaching, worship and pastoral ministry.

The third area concerns the gendered correlation between members of a faith community. Where sexual difference is honoured, then priests will make an effort to address the male T-for-G that permeates their community life and their ways of being and working together. They will recognize that women and men tend to adopt different ways both of relating and of working in groups, and will consciously move away from styles of leadership and ministry that conform to dominant male patterns and overlook or undervalue alternative models. They will try to nurture working relationships between the sexes that are mutually supportive and respectful.

The fourth and final area is concerned with the relationship between gender and personal development, both in terms of professional ministry and of spiritual formation. Part of the priestly role is to model the strong link between worship and action – in short, to 'walk the talk' of Christian commitment. So where the feminine is acknowledged and honoured, then the faith community and its clergy will uphold and encourage all its ministers in their vocation, and spiritual guides will pay attention to gendered differences, needs and vulnerabilities in the priests and others whom they support.

In each of these four areas of inquiry, I looked for stories that tell of transformation in ministry in response to the advent of a priesthood of both sexes. I set out to find more than some minor tinkering with the established order, a barely discernible nod in the direction of political correctness. Where attention is paid to sexual difference, this cannot fail to make a deep and lasting impression on the way priests – and the whole Church – do theology. So I was seeking evidence on various levels. At a cognitive level, there would be new understanding and learning that would feed into pastoral ministry. There would be those changes in attitude and outlook that come from reflection on that learning process. There would be adjustments in behaviour linked to those changes in attitude and outlook. New skills would be acquired, and working relationships would undergo some modification. There would be developments in individual and communal understanding of social responsibility. On a spiritual level, there would be new insight into gendered differences in the journey of faith, which manifests itself in vocation and ministry.

2

I have called you by name

Who am I?

I have taught many children how to play rounders, but I know
I cannot bowl a decent ball. My conviction that I'm hopeless
at throwing ensures that any attempt to do so will end in failure – usually to the amusement of any bystanders. I've always
avoided any situation where I might have to throw something
with any degree of accuracy – even training for a life-saving
certificate was fraught with the challenge of chucking a rope
usefully near the reach of any drowning person. I've constantly thought of myself as one of those typical females who just
can't throw straight.

So I was intrigued to come across an essay by Iris Marion
Young entitled 'Throwing Like a Girl'. Young notes that 'women
often approach a physical engagement with things in timidity,
uncertainty and hesitancy' (2005:43). She suggests that females
experience the body as a 'thing' to be looked at and acted upon,
distanced from the person who inhabits that body. This struck
a resonant chord in me; when it comes to handling a ball,
I have no confidence that my body will do what my brain
tells it. But that lack of self-confidence spreads into many
other areas, not only physical, and affects my sense of personal
identity.

Coming to know who we are and how we relate to the world
has a lot to do with our sex. Not just differences in physiology
and reproductive function, but a raft of gender-related factors
is at play. These factors vary from one race, culture, age or class
to another, but they are always present – in the way we dress,
the way we move, our speech, our work and so on. They shape
our self-image in every aspect of our lives, even in something
as straightforward as throwing a ball.

14

Girls from the earliest age are taught to comport themselves and to behave in particular ways. We put little girls in pretty dresses and then teach them to restrict their movements so as not to get dirty or to appear immodest. I once observed a 3-year-old on a sofa, wearing a short dress, happily bouncing around with her legs akimbo. Her mother, noticing that her daughter's knickers were on show, reminded her to 'act like a lady'. The toddler dutifully stopped her game and sat bolt upright, legs tightly together. She was being taught that her 'feminine' clothes would protect her modesty only if she restricted her bodily movements. From the cradle onwards she was learning to be circumspect about how her body looked and behaved: it must be kept in place, decorated, shaped and constrained in order to fit in with the idea of 'woman' nurtured by the culture of male T-for-G. A particular challenge for women is to find their own authentic voice, to know (as the Spice Girls say) what they really, really want and to work out how to achieve it.

It took many hundreds of years for the western Christian world to begin to recognize that women are capable of rational thought, that they benefit society by being educated, they have aspirations beyond the domestic sphere and that it is right for them to take their place in public culture. Vera Brittain, in her diaries written in the first years of the twentieth century, wrote of her heated discussions with her contemporaries about women's growing self-awareness as people in their own right. If she were to wed, she argued, she wanted a marriage of companionship rather than the role of angel or toy with whom a husband could 'soothe himself . . . after having spent the day seriously' (1982:88). She argued with a suitor who wanted her to 'learn to be a woman', maintaining that being strong and independent and developing one's intellect was in fact essentially feminine (1982:91). Brittain's ideas were pretty new, and to some shocking, at the time. But nearly a hundred years later, notwithstanding the emergence of notions about human rights, and equal opportunities, and the struggles of feminism and women's liberation, it is still the case that women's sense of identity is formed and shaped – and also constrained – by male T-for-G.

Legal, economic, social, political and religious structures have been operated according to the reason and logic of male T-for-G. Women have been locked out of the male-dominated process of forming thought, the images and symbols which order and express thought, and the culture in which those images and symbols operate. So it is hardly surprising that research into women's development of a sense of self and their spirituality has identified what Nicola Slee calls 'a profound loss of self, of authentic connection with other, and of faith' (2004:81). Many women today still struggle to adequately answer the question, 'Who am I?'

You are mine

Sophie, who has been a priest for several years, still remembers the passage from Isaiah given to her to reflect on during her diaconal ordination retreat:

> But now thus says the Lord,
> he who created you, O Jacob,
> he who formed you, O Israel:
> Do not fear, for I have redeemed you;
> I have called you by name, you are mine.
>
> (Isa. 43.1)

She recalls standing in a field and pondering these words. 'It was so resonant for me, such a revelation to know that God had called me by name.' It gave Sophie the assurance that she was right to pursue her felt vocation to priesthood, knowing that this was part of who she was, and what she really desired.

Israel's identity as a nation was intimately bound up with its formation and destiny as a people in a covenant relationship with God. From the time of their forebears Abraham and Sarah, they were the People of Promise. Similarly for Christians today, our sense of identity, both individually and in community, is formed and moulded by that covenant bond. We know ourselves to be created in the image of a loving God who knows us by name, each of us unique in nature, uniquely called to fulfil our destiny as God's children. We are part of the body of Christ, whose sense of being rests in our relationship with God and with other people. Archbishop Rowan Williams, addressing the Lambeth Conference in July 1998, spoke of 'the constantly self-critical struggle to find out who I am and who we are in and as the body of Christ'.

Our understanding of God is fundamental to the way we see ourselves, just as we can know God only from the perspective of the human self. At the same time, as we grow to maturity, we come to value ourselves as individual persons, each with our own distinct experiences, personality, gifts and vocation.

The whole Christian narrative and tradition contribute towards our sense of who we are in the world. In our worship, liturgy, prayer and Scripture, for instance, we repeatedly hear the message that we are created, loved and redeemed by God, and called to serve God by seeking to love and serve others in imitation of Jesus Christ. At the same time, our developing personhood is hugely influenced by such factors as our bio-logical makeup and the culture into which we are born. So our sex, race, nationality, social status and so on are inextricably interwoven with our sense of identity; and in turn these physio-logical and environmental factors affect the way we receive, express and pass on our faith story.

Sexual difference plays an important role in our developing sense of identity and self-worth as persons of faith. This is a particularly challenging factor in the calling and ministry of women clergy, because it is an area of conflicting beliefs and mores. Women are part of an institution that is steeped in a culture and world-view that have long been exclusively mascu-line, and in customs and rites that have been mostly male-led and sanctioned and controlled by men. Today there is only a partial acceptance within the Anglican Communion of women's priestly vocation. In this climate, it is hardly surprising that female ordinands and clergy should struggle to achieve a sense of self-affirmation, autonomy and full personhood. Sandra Schneiders, in an essay on women's spirituality, comments on the destructive and traumatic effect on Roman Catholic women of their experience of ecclesial rejection (1986:32). This sense of rejection also exists for many Anglican women who know that their sense of priestly calling is not recognized by many in their own Church family.

The priesthood carries with it a vast range of symbolic meanings associated with the nature both of God and of human beings; and here, sexual difference is at work. A male priest inherently carries with him symbolic meanings that link God with the masculine either because they are essentially male terms or because they are traditionally associated with men. Hence we are familiar with Father, King, Lord, Prince, conqueror and so on. These symbols abound in Scripture, liturgy and hymnology and come readily to the worshipper's imagination. We know God to be without gender, and yet, through our religious art and literature, we are familiar with a God who is overwhelmingly depicted as male.

The female priest causes something of a collision with this tradition. As a priest she represents God; but because we are so used to symbolizing God through the male, then there appears at first glance to be something of a 'disconnect' in symbolic meaning. Women carry a battery of diverse symbolic associations attached over millennia to the female sex. The Church from its earliest years inherited an older assumption, embedded in patriarchal culture, that the female is inferior to the male, more earthly, and needful of control. She is ritually impure and has to be kept away from holy spaces and objects, especially during menstruation and around the time of childbirth. So symbolic meanings associate the female more readily with the material rather than the spiritual, with the body rather than the intellect, with emotion rather than reason, with weakness rather than strength.

Every woman's sense of her own identity, including her perceived capacity as a focus for the presence of God, has been shaped by these learnt assumptions about the differences between men and women. Should she feel called to priesthood, then she may ask: how can someone whose sex has for so long been thought of as inferior in intelligence, rational thought and status, morally weaker and more vulnerable to temptation, be called to represent God? And if she doesn't think this of herself, she knows only too well that others are asking that sort of question. For some, the answer is that by dint of biology she cannot be a priest; this is what the Church taught for many hundreds of years. Brenda, a priest ordained fairly recently in Wales, commented to me:

> Ordination challenges our sense of identity – personal and priestly – whatever gender we are, I believe; yet I find myself wondering if, for women, there is an added dimension to this challenge, particularly on the priestly identity front, because of the people who say we cannot be priests because we are women.

As an opponent of women's ordination said at the deciding debate in the Synod in England in 1992, 'You can no more ordain a woman than a pork pie.'

Growing in confidence

Robin Greenwood wrote his book *Transforming Priesthood* in 1994, just as the first women priests in England were being ordained. While speaking hopefully of some of the changes that a priesthood of both sexes would bring about, he also notes the difficulties that many women experienced, including fear, harassment and humiliation.

Two years later came the publication of *Women Priests: The First Years*, in which editor Hilary Wakeman and other contributors tried to gauge what changes had come about in the short time since women had been admitted to the priesthood in England. Wakeman concludes that most people in the Church of England took the matter in their stride, and that 'the argument is over and done' (1996:2). Another contributor and fellow priest, Judith Rose, writes expectantly that 'changing patterns of priesthood are likely to emerge as women grow in confidence as women and in their priesthood and bring with them a new and enriching dimension to this ministry' (1996:139).

The matter of confidence in one's identity and one's abilities both as a woman and as a priest has continued to be a thorny one. A woman may struggle with coming to a sense of self, an important precursor to being in healthy relation with others. In most cultures, femininity and women's status are still not highly valued, either by society at large or by women themselves. And on the whole, these roles have not been as highly regarded or rewarded as work traditionally done by men. Researchers such as Carol Gilligan have demonstrated the widely held assumption that women on the whole tend to affiliate with and care for others more than men do, so that emotional ties are more central to many women's sense of self. Caring roles are most often done by women – looking after the vulnerable and the elderly and teaching young children, for example – and these have tended to fall to women more than men, whether these are in the home or paid jobs.

In a nutshell, more women than men ground their sense of self in nurturance and care-taking, while more men than women privilege striving to reach ambitious goals over care-taking and intimate personal relatedness. Many women struggle to address the constant demands of maintaining and nurturing those relationships, while at the same time aspiring towards self-acceptance and self-definition as autonomous individuals.

Psychotherapist Harriet Lerner comments that 'Women may participate as aggressively in their own depreciation as men' (1989:5). She finds in her practice that many women constantly belittle their own sex. I have been told myself by a female parishioner, 'I don't like women.' A colleague of mine, on telling her mother-in-law that she was entering the priesthood, was told, 'I can't see there's anything holy about a woman!' Women have started to resist the notion that assertiveness and independence, intellectual aspirations, physical prowess and sexual expression are unfeminine. Yet there are cultural pressures on women to devalue themselves, to see themselves as having secondary status, to be passive and dependent in their thinking, their language and their behaviour.

Deborah Tannen reports from a North American perspective on differences in language in men and women at work. Girls learn not to grab the spotlight, so they couch their ideas as suggestions in a working environment rather than orders, with the result that they can seem in a mixed group to be less competent and self-assured (1996:39). Women are often disliked if they make bold statements and talk with certainty. They are expected to hedge their beliefs and opinions, and seek advice from others – but this is also seen as lacking in authority (1996:170). At an international conference, I listened to a female candidate for an important office present an impressive account of herself to the assembled gathering of nearly two hundred. Later, in private, she told me how difficult she had found it to speak about herself and 'sing her own praises'. She added that she suspected this difficulty to be characteristic of many women.

Typically, women's ways of speaking may contribute to their not being listened to as much as men, but in any case women are not as likely to be listened to as men are, regardless of how they speak or what they say (1996:284). Boys, by contrast, learn to put themselves forward and emphasize the qualities that make them look good, so that they can appear to have greater confidence (1996:42). They learn more often than girls to address large groups of people, to command attention and talk authoritatively (1996:148). Tannen concludes that, in her culture, women are not meant to talk in ways that display self-confidence or draw attention. So they modify their speech, and then seem actually less self-confident than they really are (1996:38). In the workplace, if a woman takes on a role previously held by a man, then she is likely to be under suspicion as to whether she is up to the job (1996:145).

In a similar vein, Margaret Matlin cites research suggesting that women are more likely than men to prefer presenting themselves in a modest fashion to others, while men are more self-confident than women on tasks considered traditionally masculine. Matlin points out that research has not yet distin-guished whether gender differences in self-confidence are attrib-utable to women tending to be under-confident, or men being overconfident about their own abilities (2000:186). Either way, there is still cultural pressure on females to remain dependent on men, to remain passive and quiet. French writer and film maker Virginie Despentes, in *King Kong Theory*, vilifies the sort of superficial, servile, voiceless femininity that she observes in today's French culture:

> I am this sex, the one which must keep quiet, which is kept quiet. And which must take it gracefully, once again proving their harmlessness. Otherwise, you're wiped out. Men know on our behalf what we may say about ourselves. And if women want to survive they have to learn to respect this order of things.
>
> (2009:123)

Despentes argues that women must resist pandering to the way male T-for-G defines femininity and find the freedom to act as they really are. I noticed a pre-school girl wearing a T-shirt emblazoned with the slogan 'Trainee footballer's wife' – will she be encouraged to have no higher ambition than to be kept in comfort by a husband? Lerner notes that many women who come for counselling are 'unable to consciously acknowledge wishes or longings that are out of keeping with traditional feminine scripts' (1989:116). This sexual stereotyping, by a woman of herself and by others of her, can become a self-fulfilling prophecy of low self-esteem and lack of aspiration hampering her growth into maturity and full personhood – 'Girls can't throw a ball; I can't throw a ball; because I'm female I'll never learn to throw a ball properly.'

Here I am, for you called me

Hayley, currently an ordinand in training, felt a clear calling to serve the Lord from a very young age. As a girl she sang in the choir of an Anglo-Catholic church, where her faith and her love of music were nurtured. But there was also some unhappiness:

she sometimes wished that she had been born a boy so that she could serve at the altar. She grew up with a deep sense of call on her life, but with no sense of how as a female this call could come to fulfilment, except perhaps as a nun or a missionary. When she embarked on a music course, she began to worship in an evangelical charismatic Anglican church, where both she and her husband felt the call to serve God:

> There was an openness there to female ministry, but not in the ordained sense. So I tried to fulfil my sense of call in a lay capacity, serving the homeless, leading worship and Bible study groups and youth work. My husband and I then went to train for six months in a missionary training bible college, where roles were very clearly defined: women could lead intercessory groups, and speak at mixed gatherings, and lead the music side of worship, but generally leadership was male.

The couple became involved with a non-denominational independent church, where they both worked as part of the eldership in which she was the only female member. 'I was seen as lesser because I was female,' Hayley recalls. 'They felt headship was male.' So did the evangelical school where she also worked. 'When eventually I offered myself for ordination the governorship of the school refused to endorse my application, saying I was out of submission to my husband, so my references came from my very supportive Headmaster.'

It is still the case in many Anglican provinces and parishes, as well as other church communities, that even where a woman is able to offer herself for ordination, she faces certain challenges peculiar to her sex. In some cases, for instance, she may have few or no role models of her own sex to guide her. Ruby, in Britain, first felt she might have a priestly vocation at the age of eight. 'But there simply were no women priests then. So I just dismissed the idea. I knew it couldn't be.' Now a grandmother, she is currently training as a Reader but is also considering whether she is called to priesthood. Like many women, she has had to negotiate her way between a time when her experience of calling would have been unrecognized because of her sex, towards a time when it may or may not be accepted as valid in her particular case – a confusing journey which requires its own resources of endurance and self-assurance.

Chloe, following a sense of calling, also trained as a Reader, and felt similarly that God wanted her to take a further step towards ordination. 'But I always lacked confidence in my calling, which I know was to do with the way I was brought up. Even when I got to selection, I felt that I wouldn't be taken seriously.' Chloe began to develop self-confidence only during her training at theological college. Jean, an assistant priest in New Zealand, had no female priest to relate to, but she did have a very encouraging father. She commented:

> Through my life it never occurred to me that I couldn't be a woman priest – even though, when I expressed this at thirteen years old, there were no female clergy. My Dad is a priest. He's very happy about me being one too. There's always been a sense of mutual support in our spiritual journeys as a family.

Where girls and young women have had the benefit of the presence of female clergy (or sympathetic male clergy), they are likely to be more open themselves to hearing a calling to priesthood and more confident about responding. Joanna, an English woman, recalls a turning point in her life in 1977 when she attended a service in the USA, led by a female priest:

> She must have been one of the first to have been ordained priest. In the course of the next year I began to pursue a vocation towards ordination. I had already spent a good deal of time trying to discern the way forward – and had met deaconesses and parish workers – but had, thus far, not been able to recognize God's call; and believed until that moment that women's priesthood was probably 'against nature'.

Sophie is also English, born and raised as a Quaker, and like Joanna she lived and worked for some years in the USA. She became very familiar with the ministry of ordained women in the Episcopal Church. In 1992 she returned to England and taught in a girls' school.

This was the year that Synod voted to accept women as priests. I was interested that this should provoke so much difficulty, having been used to women's ministry in the States. When I offered to help the school chaplain, he very quickly asked me to preach in chapel to girls preparing for confirmation. It was he who encouraged me to seek selection.

Sophie's male colleague had discerned her calling almost before she knew about it herself, and continued to offer encouragement – something not forthcoming from all her own family. Eventually she took a post as chaplain of a girls' public school. 'I don't feel I'm a crusading figure, but I was brought up to be very independent and to know my own mind.' She finds now that, having served as a girls' school chaplain for some years, part of her ministry is to imbue the young women in her care with that sense of independence. One pupil confided to her that she was more interested in philosophy than in clothes or makeup. Sophie encouraged her to pursue her own preference rather than follow the crowd. 'I try to encourage the students in affirming their individuality, finding out who they want to be and pursuing what interests them, not just what others expect of them.'

A woman considering ordination may well have to deal with bemusement, disapproval, even hostility, simply by virtue of being female. If she perseveres with her calling she may be criticized for indulging in an 'unfeminine' degree of ambition, stridency or strong-headedness. And on top of this, the selection process will be imbued with some degree of male T-for-G which puts her at a disadvantage. One respondent told me about a deacon who was not priested with her peers 'because she was pregnant and her bishop had concerns about the status of her unborn child (was he ordaining the child too?)'. Such physiological niceties aside, most objections come in more nuanced forms. June began to pursue her calling in a diocese largely unaccepting of female priests:

In 1999, when I first put myself forward, female candidates were not allowed to see the Diocesan Director of Ordinands. We had a separate adviser for women's ministry and were kept separate throughout the process. There was still a strong assumption that you would be sponsored (if at all) for the permanent diaconate. I was steered through the process by two strong, gracious and determined women (the adviser for women's ministry and my own vocations adviser – one a deacon, the other a priest) who had stuck it out in the Diocese and won widespread respect. They were then, and remain, inspirational figures for me.

Bishop Penny Jamieson comments in *Living at the Edge: Sacrament and Solidarity in Leadership* that, in her experience, a man seeking ordained leadership is seen as responding to the call to serve. A woman in the same position is often regarded as failing to be satisfied with a life of service and inappropriately seeking after power. She recalls that the first time she sought ordination, her bishop was horrified. 'Not only was I a woman, but I was married; as he saw it, my marriage should be my exclusive preoccupation' (1997:181).

Every candidate for ordination has to meet a list of exacting selection criteria. Those in my own diocese, for example, require demonstration of a level of robustness in order to cope with the demands of training and ministry. Also stipulated are an ability to face criticism and opposition; an awareness of strengths, weaknesses and vulnerabilities; an ability to handle conflict; and a sense of integrated self and personal maturity. These are all areas that are subject to sexual difference, because our sense of identity, our way of being and knowing, is influenced by our gender. One of the clergy responsible for selecting ordinands in Wales told me he was well aware that the selection process was to some extent predicated on the assumption of the young, white, middle-class male candidate. A retired priest in England, similarly involved in the selection process, remarked, 'In my experience in the past women were often better candidates, but they were in the minority – and they had to be so much better to get selected.'

Hayley, after some years serving as an elder of an independent congregation, re-joined the Anglican Church and soon felt called to ordination. She had to face her own inner struggles, coloured by her Anglo-Catholic roots and her time in a charismatic, evangelical environment, as to whether leadership and ordained ministry should be exclusively male:

> During this time my (male) vicar was very supportive and encouraged me in my call, although he tended to think women should be non-stipendiary only and was surprised when my Diocesan Director of Ordinands told me not to put that on my form when I applied. Eventually I felt that if I did not test this call by offering myself I would be denying all that I believed God had made me for.

About this time a new rector came, who was completely supportive of Hayley and encouraged her to lead services and preach. She went to selection still believing that she would be turned down, and knowing that some of her old friends were actively praying that she would not be recommended. 'They believed I was not in God's will, and to this day they do not associate with me.' She found that the selection process was a huge endorsement of her calling. She regards the whole experience as having been completely fair and unbiased:

> I had no sense that I was treated in any way differently because I was a woman, and if anything they sought to encourage me in my identity as a female. My DDO, to my great surprise, took my sense of calling seriously and I felt respected as a Christian female leader for the first time.

Training for ministry

Having been selected, the prospective ordinand then attends a college where there may be equal numbers of women and men in training, but where most staff and others in authority are typically male. Many of these will be experienced priests who have spent most of their lives working with other men, and rarely with a superior who is female. One senior male tutor told me that the theological college in England where he worked is broadly inclusive. 'It strongly encourages gender-neutral language and makes an effort to eliminate biases (of sex, culture, sexual orientation, etc.) in its recruitment of staff or students.'

However, the organizational culture is still affected, in his experience, by the subliminal male T-for-G which 'characterizes all the mainline churches, so that anyone who is not white, male, straight and middle-class (and Oxbridge educated) is in some sense non-normative'.

The theological college which Hayley attended was, she felt, fully supportive of women's ordination, but some students were opposed to it. One year, when there was a very large and vocal group of Anglo-Catholic students, was especially difficult for her:

> They did not even want to acknowledge those of us who were female and training for priesthood, which was very difficult for me as music coordinator, as they had to work with me in the choir and with the music and musicians for all the services in college. They left last year and although there are those who still oppose women's ordination (mainly Charismatic and Evangelical ones this year) they still respect us and are friendly to us as people.

Where any minority group forms part of an institution, members of that group can feel unfamiliar with or even alienated from the mainstream culture. Eleanor, a Cambridge graduate and practising lawyer, was used to working and speaking in a mostly masculine environment, in a discursive and sometimes adversarial style. 'Entering the male-dominated institution of the church, I felt I had learnt the male language game and way of doing things, so this wasn't too difficult for me.' Brenda, before selection, had worked for twenty years in nursing, an expert in her own predominantly female field. Going to theological college as a residential student, she was aware of now being surrounded by men – a not unpleasant experience, but a markedly different culture. At that time there were only a couple of female part-time and no full-time female tutors, so she didn't have a range of same-sex priests among the staff as role models.

A senior member of staff at one English theological college told me that, within the legal obligations of equal rights legislations, every effort is made to attract female staff. 'We do all we can to make it possible for them to take up posts in the way we order the employment arrangements. I have never observed active discrimination against female applicants in the last thirteen years.' But the male T-for-G of an institution can still leave women staff and students feeling invisible or voiceless – or for some, even denigrated or disapproved of. Chloe feels that she has received great encouragement from priests with whom she has come into contact during her training for the diaconate. However, she lives in an area where there is a vocal minority of clergy opposed to women's priesthood, and she is concerned that this support may wane should she continue to train for the priesthood. 'I've done some hospital chaplaincy work, and the chaplain has been very supportive. But now I'm thinking of priesthood . . . I wonder if his attitude will change.'

Chloe couldn't recall having any training so far in gender awareness, and hadn't noticed that training staff were themselves modelling gender inclusivity in language, lecture material or worship. She told me of fellow female students who, during their training 'had a lot of hassle from male students' opposed to women's ordination: 'This went on for several months. The women were very upset. One husband wanted to come to college to complain. But when it was highlighted, the issues were resolved. It was definitely to do with gender.'

Her fellow trainee Ruby mentioned that in chapel services, 'There is one woman priest, a course leader, who uses inclusive language in preaching and in prayers. But I've never noticed any of the male staff doing it.'

The principal of an ecumenical theological college in England takes gender awareness very seriously. Jeremy spoke with me about the importance of ensuring an equal gender balance among the staff in order to reflect and model a commitment to diversity. He made a comparison with ethnicity issues: 'Recognition of difference is important. In a sense theologies of gender and embodiment follow a pattern that has been pioneered by people working in the field of ethnicity.' A generation ago, Jeremy recalled, people happily made the comment that they didn't notice differences in ethnicity – there was a sort of colour blindness. 'We've now moved beyond this, and talk about differences. But with sexual difference, there's still a gender blindness. And both forms of blindness are a cultural construct.'

The college's commitment to diversity is clearly set out in its prospectus, and there are firm protocols for dealing with incidents that fail to comply with policies. Every student has a pastoral tutor, the first port of call for any complaints or difficulties. But at a practical, everyday level, how is such a commitment encouraged, applied and monitored? Jeremy told me that he is constantly aware of these issues and tries to deal with them informally as they occur. For instance, if he hears someone telling an inappropriate joke about gender, he would discuss the matter with them in the same way that he would if he heard a racist joke. He listens to the language used in services in the college chapel:

> If in a service I hear a lot of non-inclusive language, I might talk to the people leading worship about the language they are using – 'Why were you using men and not people? Do you understand that by doing this you are excluding so many worshippers?' In marking assignments, too, I encourage care about gender – using humankind rather that man, for instance.

Jeremy constantly monitors the college's practice of inclusive-ness in this informal way, and promotes self-monitoring among the staff. 'We meet together every week and talk about pastoral issues, and any situation to do with gender that had arisen would be addressed there.' All the staff, Jeremy told me, are conscious that their role is about modelling ministry: 'It's what we call pro-social modelling – we model good practice for the students in our care by the way we respond to students and interact with them, and by the language we use.' Rather than treat gender awareness as a discrete subject, the policy of the college is to bring the issue into all aspects of the curriculum – a method Jeremy called 'vertical theming'. Gender awareness 'runs through all of college life – even to those who are invited here to lecture and to lead worship. And we certainly think it's important for students to see both men and women at the altar.'

Jeremy's establishment would be unlikely to take students opposed to women's priesthood. However, where theological colleges take female ordinands and also those who are opposed to the ordination of women, then particular pastoral and training issues arise. Eleanor found that in her college in Britain, students who opposed women priests were not allowed to air their views freely. 'I think this was a mistake because it stifled open discussion.' Ruby said that at her college, 'We have students who are Forward in Faith and won't receive Communion at the college chapel from a woman priest.' She felt very uncomfortable about what she saw as special provision being made for such students; but, she told me, the matter hasn't been opened for discussion with students in college.

In Wales there is currently a single training college, St Michael's, for the whole province. Brenda commented on her time there as a student:

> College staff seemed to have a genuine desire to be more inclusive, but the provincial selection process continued to provide students who were against women priests. So the college was trying to hold in tension and cope with strongly held and loudly vocalized beliefs while being as inclusive as possible. One of the positives for all Welsh ordinands, of whatever tradition, going to the same college is that you cannot get away from the issues women's ordination raises, especially if pro and anti ordinands are training together. I actually found this quite helpful as it reflects the reality which currently is the CiW[Church in Wales]/Anglican Communion.

The principal, Peter Sedgwick, explained that St Michael's College uses an in-house 'core skills' course, which includes a module on diversity, and which 'training incumbents would also be expected to work on'. The module examines how denominations have responded to the issue of sexuality in recent years, and considers the current framework of equality and diversity legislation with which all institutions must comply. Peter added:

The Church in Wales is currently working on 'clergy terms of service' which will become mandatory in about two to three years' time as expressions of competence. That would include an acceptance of gender equality, although of course it still allows those opposed to women's ordination to hold this position.

Ordinands are now likely to hear lectures that address appropriate relationships between the sexes. These might include how men and women can work together in ways that are mutually encouraging, how ministers of both sexes need to learn to observe careful boundaries when ministering to people of the opposite sex, and how it is essential that they avoid abusing their positions of trust and power. Similarly, ministers (usually male) offering pastoral supervision, for example during training placements, may now be given training to understand these issues.

Brenda told me of two contrasting relationships with fellow ordinands during her time of training. One was with a woman training as a permanent deacon. Throughout her time at college, Brenda found her 'very vocal about the issue of women priests. She wouldn't attend if a woman was presiding at the Eucharist.' Brenda chose not to attempt to talk with her about this matter: 'I never had a rational, reasoned conversation with her about the matter. I found the fact that she was a woman especially hard – for me her opposition felt like the ultimate betrayal.'

The other relationship was with a male student who did not recognize the priesthood of women; between them there remains an agreement to disagree and a mutually supportive friendship:

> He will phone and ask me if I'm in an OK place to talk about the issue [of women priests] – if I'm not, we don't talk about it. We support and encourage each other. We have a very close bond of friendship and mutual respect. We can talk about deeply held theological beliefs.

On her friend's invitation, Brenda attended his ordination as deacon on the afternoon of the day on which she was priested:

> As I robed I was aware of the disapproval emanating from other clergy – it felt like an invisible wall between us. I was absolutely determined to go because he had invited me. But it

was uncomfortable – I felt no huge sense of belonging in a gathering of people who were the body of Christ. Returning from Communion, in my stole, I felt proud – I held my head high and carried myself physically taller, thinking that I had every right to be there, because this is what God has called me to.

She felt that it is the mutual respect, friendship, and companionship on the journey of faith that she shares with her friend which enables them both to hold very different beliefs. This is in part, because they both acknowledge that there is pain on both sides, 'pain which we try to hold before God, seeking to not let it get in the way of our points of commonality'. At her friend's request, she is now chaplain for a voluntary organization he helps to lead.

Hayley, having previously had a great deal of discouragement in following her vocation, found her own placement a very positive experience:

> The previous incumbent had not favoured women's ordination, but the congregation were very open to it, and the new priest-in-charge, Mark, was very in favour. The church embraced me as an ordinand, as one of them. Mark viewed me as a valued 'colleague', not just as an ordinand in training. Each week I was fully involved with the life of the church, taking the role of deacon liturgically, preaching and working alongside Mark in all the occasional offices. We spent many hours in theological reflection and discussion, and I felt hugely endorsed as a person.

Pirate or pioneer?

If she continues to train successfully for the priesthood, a newly ordained clergywoman will join an institution where in many provinces she is in a pioneering role. Or, where women's priesthood has been recognized for some years, she is still more likely than not to encounter an exclusively male hierarchy: male vicar, area dean, archdeacon, bishop and so on. Additionally, her priesthood will not be recognized by a significant number of her sisters and brothers in Christ, whether clergy colleagues or laypeople. One correspondent told me that a woman ordained in the UK may be able to minister in the Diocese of Cyprus and the Gulf, with the Bishop's permission. However, all Anglican priests on the Island of Cyprus are guests in an Orthodox country and great care is taken not to antagonize their hosts by 'acting unwisely in any respect'. This means a woman priest would not celebrate the Eucharist in a building which belongs to the Orthodox Church, but is able to work in whatever capacity she is licensed for in other buildings designated as 'Anglican churches'. A licensed woman priest with the Bishop's Permission to Officiate in the Paphos Chaplaincy commented that she has a good working relationship with readers and priests in the chaplaincy and across the diocese, and finds that:

> The Cypriot people themselves are quite intrigued that I am a woman in a dog collar. They ask what it means – and I tell them – and many express thoughts that it could be very good for them to do the same. And some of them come and join us at our services – Songs of Praise in the park and carols at Christmas.

To enable others fully to flourish in their Christian life, any priest needs to feel fairly secure in his or her own sense of identity and calling, and to feel accepted as someone with a calling to ordained ministry within a given community. The rub here for female priests is that, in many provinces, dioceses and parishes, we are uncertain as to whether in fact we are welcome. Training institutions may have developed regulations and policies about gender inclusiveness, but newly ordained deacons and priests may find that the enlightened culture of theological college is not necessarily reflected in their training parishes or among their colleagues in ministry. These challenges, all peculiar to female clergy, may be compounded by a learnt sense of self that tells a woman either that, as a woman, she is inferior, subordinate and secondary in status and ability, or that others around her believe this to be so, or that to strive against such ingrained attitudes would mark her out as unfeminine.

On the one hand, female clergy are being encouraged to 'be themselves', to make their own distinct contribution towards the ministry of the Church. On the other hand, some fellow

Christians do not accept who they are, and offer a response to them that can range from measured disagreement to outright hostility. Great hurt has been felt on both sides of the debate. Fr Geoffrey Kirk, writing on the Forward in Faith website in 2004, criticizes the Windsor Report for papering over the cracks of what he calls 'the continuing crisis over the ordination of women' across the Anglican Communion (19 October 2004). He argues that the provinces of Canada, the USA and Australia in particular failed to provide adequately for dissentients and fears that 'the pirates are determined to take over the ship by any means, and that there is no one at the helm to repel boarders'. Such provocative language is not uncommon in the debate around women's ordination; and when opposition expresses itself too belligerently, whether in words or action, individual women themselves experience degrees of intimidation and humiliation.

Eleanor spoke of her shock at the contrast between her previous working environment in secular employment and her new position as a curate. 'In my old law firm there was mutuality and respect – people were aware of gender but it was not an issue. The Church is an alien medieval world by comparison.' For a number of clergywomen, however much they sense the validity of their God-given calling, there is still hurt and disappointment at the lack of wholehearted affirmation by the Church which they love and serve. This can show itself in small but significant ways. When Eleanor was a curate, her male incumbent did not challenge blatantly sexist remarks made by parishioners. 'I was told not to make a fuss. And of course if you do say anything, you're just a stroppy woman.' Eleanor recalled a diocesan committee of which she was the sole female member. A senior layman, during a discussion about a vacancy in the diocesan office, commented that, of course, they would not want to employ a woman of childbearing age:

> I was horrified and challenged his remark. All the men just looked at the table. It would have been much better if one of the men said something – certainly the male cleric. This sort of behaviour would have been unthinkable in the law firm where I used to work.

Brenda's incumbent talks with her and other colleagues about what was being said by those actively opposing women's priesthood:

> He'll report these things in a light-hearted way – but sometimes I would rather not know. He told me about a man in the congregation who asked him who was taking Stations of the Cross. When he found out it was me, he said that he would come because 'she can do that – it's not sacramental'. To me, it seemed that as a traditionalist the man was ignoring an understanding of ontological change in ordination. This was something I felt very strongly at my ordination. I will always be a priest, no matter what I do. I and others have seen the effect of that change in me. That parishioner has been rude to me on other occasions – disrespectful to me as a human being, let alone as a woman and a priest.

Brenda gets on very well with her vicar, and for most of the time gender issues take up little of her attention. But on this occasion she did wonder why he didn't challenge that parishioner. 'I think he is not always aware of the impact that [this behaviour] can have on me personally.' During her time as his curate, Brenda has attempted to have conversations with him relating to gender issues, but she has found that, on the whole, these have been unsatisfactory from her perspective. The result is, she says:

> I have chosen not to talk with him about such matters – I say to myself that he doesn't do gender, and to raise the matter wouldn't be productive in our otherwise very good relationship. I doubt if he has any inkling of how deeply I feel at times about the negative comments he reports on, and how they impact on me personally.

Emmanuelle, who has ministered both in England and in Australia, spoke of some difficulties, 'especially [with] older men who in their working life were not used to women being in "higher" roles'. She has found that this has led to 'patronizing words (and sometimes actions)' and a 'clash of "authority" when men were used to women acquiescing/obeying'. She also reports incidents of men attempting to 'use physical intimidation and bullying to dominate and overwhelm'. By contrast, she has found that many laywomen have commented on 'the joy they feel at having a priest who is a woman, especially when she is obviously a woman: takes care of her hair, makeup, dresses like a woman not a pseudo-male'.

Women have to face particular questions about physical appearance. The priesthood has always been delineated by some form of recognizable dress, in terms of vestments, collars and colours. Ordained women, like police officers, soldiers and firefighters, have had to adopt an essentially male uniform. Jim Cotter, priest and writer, told me he felt sympathy with the dilemma clergywomen may feel in wanting to 'fit in' with a male-dominated priesthood and their traditional uniform while also wanting to remain creative and feminine in their mode of dress. He recalled attending a service in California where a female presbyter was not only wearing liturgical green vestments but also sporting green fingernails. For him this was off-putting because it detracted from his focus on worship. For women particularly, there is a fine distinction to be made between remaining feminine in one's demeanour and drawing too much personal attention.

With such a raft of obstacles and constraints to negotiate, a newly trained clergywoman must find deep resources in her sense of identity, and develop a strong sense of self-worth and security so as to withstand outright non-acceptance or more nuanced forms of hostility. Additionally, in all but the few provinces where women clergy have now ministered for a generation, she inevitably has to face the challenge of a landscape with very few points of reference for women, because they have occupied this space for so short a time. Geraldine was ordained seven years ago in the Liverpool diocese and has since moved to the Middle East because of her husband's job. She described Abu Dhabi as 'a wonderful place to live out my calling and ministry as a priest, which I know will help and direct my ministry in to the future when we eventually leave'. However, she said:

> It isn't always easy. Many people who come to worship have no experience of women priests apart from negative misconceptions ... It's probably not dissimilar to how it was for women newly ordained to the priesthood in the 90s in the UK.

Peter Clark wrote a generation ago of his belief that women were drawing the attention of the Church to 'areas of thinking and feeling without which our understanding of God and of humanity must be incomplete' (Furlong 1984:189). At the same time, he was worried that in the years ahead, female clergy would become subsumed into the rigid institution of the established churches, so that their distinctive contribution as women would be lost. Others, in seeing first-hand the distinctive and invaluable contribution women are making in the Christian community, have changed their minds about the priesthood of women. One man I met told me that he had been an 'archetypical male – single-sex public school, Oxbridge' for whom the ordination of women was so far from his radar that he would not receive communion from a woman. Initially he worked in a very masculine environment, but later he found himself working almost entirely with women, both as a chaplain and in his specialism in healthcare:

> I had two female chaplaincy colleagues, a Roman Catholic nun and an Anglican deacon, and of course neither could offer Eucharistic ministry. I was the only one who could, even in our entirely female context in a women's hospital. I began to think as a theologian that this just didn't make sense.

This man now trains women and men for Christian ministry, and is keen to promote awareness of sexual difference among his students.

Culture, race, gender

St John's Cathedral claims proudly to be the first in the world to greet the new day. Its white tower dominates the skyline of the largely low-rise city of Napier in the North Island, New Zealand. Designed in the modernist style, it was erected on the ruins of the previous building which collapsed when an earthquake struck in 1931 during a service of Holy Communion. The Waiapu diocese is committed to Tikanga Rua, the partnership with Maori built on justice and respect, and the cathedral incorporates a Maori memorial chapel decorated with Maori craftwork. The diocese promotes the Church as 'welcoming and inclusive of all, open, broad-based and ecumenical in its understanding of the Christian faith'. The first Maori Bishop of Waiapu was appointed in 1928, and the first Anglican female priests were ordained in 1977. So an entire generation has now been brought up with the experience of inclusive ministry in terms of gender, race and culture.

When I met the Dean, the Very Reverend Helen Jacobi, and some fellow clergywomen for dinner at Helen's home overlooking the cathedral, it seemed to me that the broad aspiration to be welcoming and inclusive of all was palpably evident. I came away with the impression that on the whole, in this diocese, clergy have come to honour one another's differences while offering mutual support and respect. Helen was the first woman to be appointed dean, and she felt that nowhere in New Zealand was women's priesthood really in question. Her remarks chimed with Penny Jamieson's conclusion that, in this province, 'There is little of the rhetoric of gender bias around these days, and women do not interpret a refusal [at selection] as attributable to their gender' (1997:51).

Another guest at dinner was Dorothy Brooker, who in 2005 was elected the first female Minister General of the Third Order of the Society of St Francis dispersed in the Americas, Europe, Africa, Australia and Aotearoa New Zealand. She cautioned that there were still 'a few ripples', but that on the whole the matter of female priests was no longer an issue. Now every diocese in the province of Aotearoa, New Zealand and Polynesia accepts women priests and bishops. But Dorothy conceded that it had not been easy for the pioneers:

> Some of the first women priests tried to be more like their male counterparts and came across as too aggressive – or else they were too 'feminine' and put people off. This was in the 1970s, of course, when there was all that pressure for women to measure up to the Superwoman role model.

Dorothy and other women of her generation round the table felt that the history of women's suffrage in New Zealand had nurtured and encouraged them, and given them confidence to pursue their calling. Many Pakeha women (those of European descent) arrived in New Zealand determined to leave behind the oppressions of Victorian Britain and to weave together a new, more egalitarian society. Christian women – mostly Anglican, Roman Catholic, Methodist and Presbyterian, and often hardy and outspoken people – were active in supporting the interests of the Maori and the indigenous church and culture. They also fought for women's rights, and in 1893 New Zealand became the first country in the world to give equal voting rights to both sexes. Yet the Church continued to teach women to be submissive and passive in an aggressively male-dominated, go-getting society. Sue Adams, in an article entitled 'Towards Partnership: Race, Gender and the Church in Aotearoa-New Zealand', writes: 'The church, with its male god and its theology of maleness, pushed women out of the places of actual decision-making, out of effective theological focus, out of the public sphere, and into a private preserve of women's space' (Heyward and Phillips 1992:93).

Women continued to struggle to be heard against the established culture, and eventually New Zealand became one of the first Anglican provinces to ordain female priests, and then in 1989 to elect a female bishop. This history and background goes a long way to explain the sense of assurance and self-confidence I observed amongst female clergy in Wellington and Waiapu. Dorothy commented, 'I know I have a strong sense of identity and self-worth,' and she recalled an incident that had occurred when she was invited to preach during a service in England:

> A man walked in before the service and saw that a woman was to be the preacher and walked straight out. I said, 'He will miss a good sermon,' with ripples of laughter by those around me. Having that confidence in myself allowed me to take these things in my stride.

Ros and Jean are associate priests in the parish of St James, Lower Hutt, in the neighbouring diocese of Wellington. The parish has a male vicar, two female associate priests and several honorary assistant clergy of both sexes, among them Penny Jamieson, retired bishop. Its website lists mutual respect, recognizing differences and being a caring and supportive environment as values that the parish promotes. Ros told me that she had found no resistance to female priests during her time in the parish. 'I've no experience of opposition to a woman. There have been several female priests at St James before me, including Penny, who was a curate here.' The current vicar is very supportive of women clergy, as is their Bishop, and Ros herself has never heard any negative comments from clergy colleagues. Jean agreed that in her region any resistance to women in a priestly role is rare, and she has never experienced it from clergy colleagues.

The Church in South Africa has similarly faced challenges of embracing differences in race and culture as well as gender. Jane had a struggle in her first incumbency in Natal with differing notions of leadership:

> The parish was undergoing a swift transformation at the time. It had been a conservative white suburb and by the time I arrived the neighbourhood was more mixed in racial composition . . . There was a lot of tension.
>
> One lay minister insisted that the parish needed 'strong leadership': I struggled with her comment because I was young and inexperienced, but also committed to a style of leadership that is collaborative, community-minded and empowering (power decentralized and more people involved and contributing). I told her that if she meant that she needed someone to tell her what to do and think all the time, then that wasn't the kind of leader that I was.

David Bannerman, now Bishop of the Highveld, first came there in 1995, having previously been in a diocese which did not ordain women. So working with female clergy was 'a learning curve for me':

> From my perspective as a white man, I can see that our communities – black and white – are patriarchal in many respects, and our theology has colluded with that. We are living in a society which is a result of the abolition of apartheid and where there is freedom with our constitution. But there is tension between the constitution – perhaps a bit before its time – and what is being lived out. Women may have to work through that, and for black women, there are deeper issues to overcome, perhaps especially in rural areas.

Bishop David, in appointing clergy to posts in his diocese, has to 'look at cultural and racial compatibility as well as gender. Is the synergy going to be right?' One appointment that caused some consternation was that of Alice, who became rector in a community where women's ordination was vehemently opposed by some parishioners. Alice commented:

> I entered the parish fairly reluctantly and fearfully at the encouragement of three male churchwardens who believed it to be a good move for the parish. The male assistant priest at the time had been in the parish for 25 years, and was vocally opposed to the ordination of women. My advent into the parish was controversial to say the least, but by the grace of God, and through careful journeying with the assistant priest and congregation, I found myself at the end of my first five years as one of the very few people the assistant priest would allow to journey with him during a particularly arduous battle with cancer. He subsequently trusted me with all the responsibility of his funeral and disposal of his assets after his death.

Alice found the gradual acceptance of her ministry, by her parish and by her assistant priest, a humbling experience, and one that, she said, 'showed how God works miracles when we gently engage with those who previously regarded us as "the enemy"'. Following the death of the assistant priest, Alice's next curate was 'one of the women who had opposed my appointment, and we have become firm friends since her ordination to the priesthood'.

A genealogy of affirmation

Jung Chang recalls in *Wild Swans* (1992) that her grandmother was one of the first generation of females in China to be given a name. The author told me that her great-grandmother was simply called by the family name, together with a female suffix to that name. When I asked Jung Chang how she thought it must have felt for women to be without their own names, she equated it with the low status of females in Chinese society, and to the old adage that 'Women have long hair and short intelligence'.

What's in a name? Well, a great deal, according to our narrative of faith. We cannot overestimate the affirmation and sense of 'belongingness' we experience when God assures us that 'I have called you by name, you are mine' (Isa. 43.1). Names carry the power to affirm and transform – just as the lack of a name is uniquely disempowering. At baptism we are welcomed by name into the family of the Church. In Scripture names are given to children to denote a special identity or destiny. Hagar is told by an angel to name her son Ishmael, 'for the LORD has heard of your misery' (Gen. 16.11). The Lord tells King David to name his son Solomon, a word sounding in Hebrew very like the word for peace, because 'I will give peace and quiet to Israel in his days' (1 Chron. 22.9). Following the angel Gabriel's instructions to Zechariah, Elizabeth confirms at her son's circumcision that he is to be named John. Names are changed, too, so as to mark a new chapter or particular calling. God changes Abram's name to Abraham, 'for I have made you the ancestor of a multitude of nations' (Gen. 17.5). Jesus gives Simon the name Peter (meaning rock), 'and on this rock I will build my church' (Matt. 16.18). Saul becomes Paul following his conversion.

St Matthew's Gospel begins with a genealogy giving the descent of Jesus from Abraham, through King David, through the time of the Exile, and finally through Joseph. The long list omits Mary and every other foremother of Jesus, except for four females: Tamar, Rahab, Ruth and Bathsheba. Each of these very different women has something in common with Mary of Nazareth: they are all agents in taking forward God's messianic plan. Tamar, to gain justice, abandons her widow's garments and waits by the road for her father-in-law Judah. She becomes a forebear of Boaz (Gen. 38.14). Rahab saves her family by harbouring Joshua's spies and joining the Israelites (Josh. 2.2). Ruth finds a new husband and home in Boaz, and becomes a great-grandmother to David (Ruth 3.7). Bathsheba is widowed by King David, to whom she then bears the child Solomon (2 Sam. 11.4).

Something else they have in common is that they all risk condemnation by standing outside the norms of contemporary patriarchal society where women are marginalized and their behaviour strictly controlled. Rahab is a prostitute, and Tamar pretends to be one. Ruth is a poor foreigner and a childless widow. Bathsheba, newly widowed, unites herself with the king who engineered the death of her husband Uriah. Mary becomes pregnant out of wedlock, during her year of betrothal to Joseph. All these women form a part of the messianic story which culminates in the Incarnation.

In the Nativity story, we hear that Joseph's reaction to Mary's revelation is to seek a quiet divorce. But, in obedience to God's prompting, he stays with her and supports her through pregnancy and childbirth, so that God's messianic purposes can be fulfilled. Joseph supplies the moral and practical support and protection that Mary needs in order to carry forward God's plan as it unfolds in radically new ways through her son. Jesus her son will go on to cross all sorts of boundaries and challenge many preconceived ideas about the nature of God's Kingdom.

In the history of the Church, not least in the last generation or so, pioneering women, in the footsteps of their Israelite foremothers, have stepped outside traditional boundaries so as to pursue God's call to build the Kingdom. Women have added their names to the long genealogy of apostolic succession, often in the face of condemnation and hostility from fellow Christians. Robin Gurney, in a report on women in the churches of Europe, comments on women's lack of self-esteem and confidence, and challenges men to help women take advantage of opportunities and responsibility. 'Opening [the doors] is not enough. Women often experience a passive acceptance of their claims but not an active support' (1997:31).

For a priesthood of both sexes fully to represent the whole Church, and to be fully effective in its ministry, the Church needs a prophetic Mary-*and*-Joseph partnership. In order to name ourselves as priests called by God and fully recognized by the people of God, women need to encounter not just passive tolerance but positive acknowledgement and active, practical affirmation and support from our brothers and sisters in Christ.

3

Being mindful in God-talk

Renewing an old symbolic order

One of the first services I went to at the theological college I attended was led by a Nonconformist minister. I can't remember now whether it was a eucharistic service or what he preached on, but I have a very strong memory about the words he used. The hymns, the Scripture, his sermon, the prayers – all were in language that included me as a woman.

I had grown up reciting the Book of Common Prayer. I had read *Pilgrim's Progress* and sung 'He who would valiant be' and 'When a knight won his spurs' and tried hard to identify with those male models of discipleship. I had struggled with Scripture that never seemed to address me personally. I had learnt in private reading of Scripture to change a few pronouns to try and encounter more directly the presence of God in my life. I had chafed against the old assumption that in language 'man embraces woman', because that just didn't work for me. In one parish I had appealed unsuccessfully for the language of worship material to be made more gender-neutral. But in all those years, I had never before actually taken part in a service that used entirely inclusive language. It was electrifying. I left feeling both elated and distressed: elated to feel so embraced and accepted in the body of Christ, and distressed that I had had to wait so long for this experience, and then not in the context of my own confession.

The rather uncomfortable mix of feelings stayed with me during my years of ministerial training as I struggled to find my own identity as a female ordinand. I was preparing to enter a male-dominated hierarchy whose culture was in many ways alienating to me and which itself was not wholly comfortable with my femininity. Part of this struggle had to do with the spoken and written language of worship, but it ran much deeper than that. The heart of the problem was to do with how I reconciled being a woman with being a priest; and that meant thinking about the wealth of symbols attached both to priesthood and to woman.

Clergy bear the authority of the Church to offer the ministry of word and sacrament, and provide leadership in worship, to proclaim the gospel, to teach and guide those in their care and to encourage others in their faith. At the same time they carry an array of symbolic meanings associated not only with their priestly vocation but also with their particular sex. And the ordained woman carries age-old symbolic meanings that appear at variance with the priestly role. Hence in women's priesthood there is apparently, as I noted earlier, something of a 'disconnect' in symbolic meanings.

Women have always been associated with the earthly and natural, with impurity and bodiliness, with the private and domestic, with passivity and subservience. From at least the time of Aristotle in ancient Greece, scholars taught that a woman's biology made her defective: a female child was misbegotten, and deficient in powers of reasoning. The Church Father Tertullian, admonishing women to dress modestly, told them that they were the devil's gateway, descendants of Eve and therefore the first deserters of the divine law.

From then on, various pronouncements from the church establishment restricted women's access to sacred objects and spaces on the grounds of their impurity, especially during menstruation. In the fourth century, the Council of Laodicea banned women from entering the altar area. Women were offered the example of Mary as the epitome of obedience, the eternal and sinless virgin. Thus was she set apart from all other women, alone of all her sex, an impossible ideal of saintly womanhood beyond the aspiration of any flesh-and-blood mortal, as perfect as she was inaccessible, her sexuality reduced to an implication. The so-called sexual lust of real women was being given as grounds for accusations of witchcraft. The Reformer Martin Luther taught male dominance and extolled obedience to men, marriage and motherhood as the proper role for women who, he wrote, had 'lots of filth and little wisdom'.

Western philosophers in the nineteenth century warned against females being educated because it upset the natural order. Medical experts cautioned against educating girls because it could lead to hysteria; allowing women any more human rights was likely to make them ill. There were strict limits on which subjects were suitable for girls. Elizabeth Blackwell, born in 1821 in England, was the first woman to qualify as a medical doctor in New York in 1849. But she endured a great struggle to find a college that would accept her, and even then, she was barred from classroom medical demonstrations, on the grounds that they were inappropriate for a woman. In 1878, the Society of Apothecaries decided to make an award to young women for the study of botany – this subject being deemed fit for the female mind.

With all this weight of history, any woman contemplating a call to ordination might reasonably wonder how the notions of woman and priesthood can be reconciled. For me the answer came in understanding how the woman priest is able, simply in her being, to subvert outdated and prejudicial culturally constructed associations and to open up new symbolic possibilities. If women carry symbolic associations with bodiliness and earthliness, then a woman priest invites us to see that God is immanent in the concrete world of real human beings, and all created things. If a priest is female, then she shows us that women as well as men are made fully in the image of God, and that God's presence can be mediated as much through the female as through the male. If women have historically been associated with impurity, then the woman priest is subverting the age-old belief that women are essentially unclean and need to be kept away from holy spaces and objects. If women were always assumed to be inferior and passive in nature, then the woman priest is overturning that assumption by taking on a role of public leadership and responsibility, and challenging the old order that banished women to voicelessness. If women were kept away from sacred roles and places, then the female priest reclaims that sacred space for all women, and begins to furnish it with the wisdom of women's ways of being and knowing.

It follows that a priesthood of both sexes affirms sexual difference: women and men are equal, but not exactly the same, since each brings different qualities and values which the feminine and the masculine symbolize. To be a priest is more than simply doing a job: it is about who I am, the essence of my identity as a person and as a child of God. All the more reason, then, why the Church should not expect a female priest to be and to act as if she were an honorary man. She has her own distinct experience and way of knowing, her own way of responding to the sacred and to the world, and of living her faith. One woman's experience may be vastly different from another's, and there is no monolithic model for all women any more than there is for all men. But recent research across many cultures and communities has pointed up the presence of sexual difference, and the way that it has been ignored by male T-for-G.

We can see this in so many aspects of society: in the workplace, the law, industry, government, religion. Male T-for-G is so obviously the norm that it is often taken to be the only way that the world can possibly be. We assume that an organizational culture, its language and ways of behaving, will be a men's culture. Even scientific knowledge, supposedly objective and neutral, is subject to the same male bias. Until recently, even when sociologists analysed organizational cultures, they often overlooked their 'maleness'. So studies have investigated, for instance, the culture of institutions, communities and rituals, but the matter of gender was largely ignored. Females remained muted, if not silent, in the data collected and in subsequent analysis and interpretation. As anthropologist Dale Spender puts it, 'Men have made up the meanings for society and then have checked with other men to see if those meanings are accurate' (1980:76). Spender looks at various ways, some obvious and others very subtle, that masculine language mutes and marginalizes feminine experience. She maintains that 'If women were to gain a public voice, they would in many instances supply very different meanings from those which have been provided, and legitimated, by men' (1980:78).

The great strength of a priesthood of both sexes is that it has the potential, in a way that is impossible for a single-sex priesthood, to bring to Christian life and worship all the gendered ways of being and symbolic meanings that attach both to the divine and to humanity. Such a priesthood is able to offer a symbolic focus for the sacramentality of the female body and for women's ways of being in the world which have until now been largely ignored and overlooked. A priesthood that includes women offers symbolic space for all women in a previously masculine symbolic order.

For some women, especially where they are in a pioneering position, the possibility of beginning to explore sexual difference by breaking open this old symbolic order may still be some way off. June is a non-stipendiary priest ministering in an English parish. She says:

> None of the parishes in which I have so far served has reached the stage of taking sexual difference seriously . . . In all three I have been the first woman priest to serve there, and two of the parishes have a fairly recent history of opposition to women clergy. So they haven't yet got past the stage of relief that a woman priest is not such a radical departure as some had feared. It's the similarity, not the difference, that is being affirmed . . . So, if transformation is happening (and I sense that it probably is) it's still very much at a subconscious level and has yet to be fully articulated or even acknowledged.

June's experience will be a familiar one to many clergy, where congregations still need to be reassured about the unity and appropriateness of the priesthood of both sexes before tapping into its diversity. But for others, the presence of women priests has allowed for opportunities to explore and develop the implications of sexual difference in preaching and interpretation of Scripture, in language and liturgy, in prayers and hymns and in pastoral ministry.

In the Highveld, South Africa, one way that sexual difference is honoured is simply in the mode of address used for priests. It is the custom there to address female priests as 'Mother'.

Bishop David told me, 'We say Mother to reflect the mother-hood as well as the fatherhood of God. It seems a fairly straight-forward and obvious corollary to the male Father.' Alice, a priest in the same diocese, comments that the title 'Mother' is a term of respect, 'especially where people have been conditioned through their culture and upbringing to respect others in this form' (she is also sometimes called 'Mama Alice'). Although ambivalent about the title herself, she feels that it gives female priests in her diocese a better sense of inclusion, 'almost as if we are then taken more seriously, which can be a real difficulty in a room full of men, some of whom are still reluctant to accept the ordained priesthood of women'.

The process of becoming sensitized to sexual difference has been helped by the fact that the increase in women priests has coincided with a growth in the contribution of feminist the-ology to disciplines such as biblical scholarship, hermeneutics, liturgical studies and so on. Of course, male priests can be sensitive to gender in these areas, just as some female priests may lack such awareness. But on the whole, these issues are more likely to be addressed where worshipping communities are served by priests who include women, the sex which has for so long remained voiceless and unrepresented.

The Eucharist

Those working on liturgical renewal in recent years have given thought to every aspect of worship – from gesture and posture to vestment and seating. Now that the Anglican Church has a priesthood of both sexes, and with the rise of feminist con-sciousness, the liturgical movement has increasingly shown an awareness of sexual difference in providing relevant, meaning-ful and life-enhancing worship.

The Eucharist is the central Anglican rite where the narrative of faith is retold and re-enacted and the community of disciple-ship is renewed and moulded. It is laden with symbols that, as long as they continue to bear significance for the contemporary worshipper, are empowering and life-changing. Presiding priests have a key symbolic function here, not only in what they say and do but also in their very presence, in what they stand for in representing both God and Christ and the people of God. Where women and men celebrate at the same altar, then the broad raft of symbols associated with each sex is incorporated into the symbolic language of priesthood. Rebecca's comment is probably true of any number of female priests:

> I'm not sure that there's anything I deliberately *do* 'as a woman' in celebrating liturgy. But I am certainly conscious that I *am* a woman and that I look and sound different from male colleagues . . . it's more to do with my consciousness of my *being*, which is a being that is by nature different from a male being.

With a priesthood of both sexes, we can see more clearly that both female and male bodies can mediate the presence of God, and that God can be approached and expressed equally through the feminine and the masculine. To acknowledge and explore this greater range of symbolic meaning is to broaden and enrich our worship, our relationship with God and our understanding of ourselves as members of the body of Christ.

Sometimes it might be simply the presence of a female celebrant that can have a transformative effect in worship, on worshippers, and on pastoral issues. June, a curate in a London parish, told me:

> I was attending the early morning service, which has always been exclusively male in its celebrants and servers. When I approached the communion rail, the vicar opened it up and invited me inside, and then handed me the chalice. I asked him afterwards why he had done this and he told me that he had been approached by a lesbian couple to ask if they would be welcome at this church. He assured them that they would, but then decided that he couldn't say that with integrity if women were still excluded from the sanctuary. So now he wants me to take part whenever I'm there.

All priests are in the business of birthing. We learn from Jesus that we have to be reborn into our new lives in Christ. The priest has a recognized role in 'midwifing' others to that new life and caring for them as they mature in faith. The female priest at the altar visibly and audibly signifies the feminine, the maternal, with many associations around procreation, birth-giving and caring. These are all symbols associated with the life-giving, nurturing God, but which are given particular resonance when borne in the body of a female priest. It is a symbolism that comes alive in a priesthood of both sexes: visibly present in the woman, by virtue of her sex, yet also carried by the man, in the sense that he honours it in his recognition, as Christ did in using the birthing metaphor to talk to Nicodemus about faith. Speaking about presiding at the Eucharist, a male colleague commented to me, 'It's the closest a bloke gets to giving birth.'

Gill, ordained in the diocese of Natal, South Africa, commented on the powerful symbolism of her own pregnancies following her ordination:

> Both my pregnancies served as a powerful visual reminder of the motherhood of God. My bishop at the time spoke to me once about being in New York in the 1980s. He was very anti-women's ordination at the time and remembered going to a service and watching the altar party come down the aisle and the priest's pregnant stomach was the first sign of her. He changed his mind in those years in New York.

Many women priests have come across communicants who refuse to accept Holy Communion from their hand, in the belief that a woman's biology renders her incapable of priesthood. But Edidah-Mary Mujinya, a priest and canon in the diocese of West Ankole, Uganda, told of communicants actively searching her out at the altar rail:

> When I was still a deacon, I used to assist in our Cathedral. During Holy Communion some people would dive to get to the side where I was giving the chalice. They seemed to feel more blessed being served by a woman clergy even when still a deacon. [They had] a realization that God's work could be performed by whoever God sends for his own glory . . . they just felt a kind of special blessing upon them as they were to get it from a rare minister (a woman priest) – this implying that they trusted that a female is equally anointed for service as men are.

In the Foreword to Robert Hovda's book on eucharistic liturgy, *Strong, Loving and Wise*, Godfrey Diekmann recalls that in previous years, priests were taught not to allow 'personal emotion or interpretation to find expression in their actions. There was to be nothing "subjective". Their ideal was to remain "the faceless priest"' (1976:v). Diekmann finds this to be a wrong assumption, because the priest is not a nerveless automaton but a human agent who is called to bring worship to life for the benefit of the community. These days, each priest, over time, finds his or her own 'style' in presiding at the Eucharist.

The first wave of women priests, joining an exclusively male-led institution, had no role models of their own sex to follow. But over the years, as they have brought their own life experience and way of knowing into the priesthood, they have ways of presiding and leading that sit comfortably and meaningfully with their own bodies and approach to worship. In *Presiding Like a Woman* (2010) editors Nicola Slee and Stephen Burns gather together the contributions of a number of writers, priests and laypeople, female and male, to address the question of what it means to preside like a woman, and the significance of bodily matters such as gesture and voice. In my own contribution ('Being and Becoming: How the Woman Presider Enriches Our Sacred Symbols') I argue for eucharistic worship that pays attention to gender by recognizing and honouring feminine aspects of God and God in the feminine.

The priest's voice is a vital instrument in worship, and inevitably, where male and female priests are heard, there will be a range of tone, pitch and timbre, and this will touch worshippers in a number of ways, as well as offering variety. One woman commented after a service that she felt my voice spoke to her of 'compassion'. Other female priests have mentioned receiving similar comments about this quality in their voices. Rebecca commented of her own voice that it is to do with tone. 'Sometimes I think that my tone of voice is warmer than the tone that some men use.' She felt that she often allowed 'a greater sense of personal intimacy to seep through my presiding than some male priests might be comfortable with . . . I do think that the Eucharist is a very intimate act – it's about connections and going beyond our usual boundaries.'

Each priest adopts a particular way of doing the 'manual acts' of taking, blessing, breaking and giving. The tradition has been for the celebrant to focus directly and solely on the elements. But some people favour a more 'horizontal' approach to include the worshipping community. Sasha told me:

> I've always watched the way priests officiate at the Communion and I've noticed that most people seem to have their eyes closed, or look heavenwards or only at the elements etc. when presenting them. I tend to look directly at the congregation, moving the chalice from left to right, making eye contact if they're looking at me. *This is my body which is given for you* . . . For me this is all about a personal relationship with God and what Jesus did for each one of us and so I do try to personalize it.
>
> I suppose I'm hoping that people will realize that this isn't just something historical that happened a long time ago, but that each time we re-enact the Last Supper we are drawn into a personal communion with Christ today, and in their vulnerable state I hope they feel Jesus reaching out to them. I've never seen anyone else do this. I suspect it is quite a 'feminine' thing to do – I've never really thought about it before, it's just something that has evolved, and feels right.

Dawn, vicar of a parish in New Zealand, noticed differences in the way the ablutions are carried out. Her remarks accord (consciously or otherwise) with the feminist liturgical principle of seeking as worship leader to stand not above or apart but alongside the congregation:

> Some clergy prefer to conduct ablutions after the Eucharist at/ on the table/altar, whereas others prefer to 'do the washing up' off to one side, on the credence table. It is my observation that as a generalization women prefer the former, and men the latter. I wonder if this reflects a differing theology whereby for women we are gathering together for a meal amongst friends – almost as though we are gathering around the kitchen table to eat, and therefore setting up and clearing up on the altar is entirely appropriate – whereas for men we are the guests at a dinner and the

polite thing is for the dirty dishes to be whisked away and dealt with out of sight. I personally have a strong preference for treating the congregation as family friends rather than guests, and as a result everything I do is done on the table/altar for all to see.

Searching for holy women

In the English church where I served as deacon, there was a mid-week Eucharist in the Lady Chapel for a small congregation almost entirely made up of retired folk who were also Mothers' Union members. Once a month intercessory prayers focused on the Mothers' Union worldwide. The vicar asked me to lead some of the services and to prepare a series of sermons for them. In his own sermons, he liked to tell stories about saints, using them as models for Christian living. What struck me about the stories he told was that every saint he preached on was male, while the congregation was almost exclusively female. I wondered whether the women had ever heard stories about female saints or other women, and whether they had heard those stories interpreted in their own, local, contemporary context. With this question in mind, I set about devising a series of sermons that told of the lives of female saints and other women who could offer realistic role models for today's women in their own everyday lives.

I soon realized that one challenge in this undertaking was the imbalance between male and female saints. In the Church of England lectionary, the number of female saints I could choose from was much smaller than of male saints. There is no single calendar of saints across the Anglican Communion: each province has its own, adapted to its local situation, focusing on its own important historical figures. But the dearth of female figures seems to occur across many provinces. Elizabeth J. Smith, writing from a North American perspective, comments that 'celebrations of holy men outnumber those of holy women by more than two to one in the Episcopal Church's calendar' (1999:125).

I've made a cursory tally of commemorated saints, bishops, missionaries, apostles, pastors, martyrs, abbots, poets and teachers in my current Church in Wales lectionary for the days between Easter and Pentecost. It shows a proportion of about ten males to one female. Of the women listed throughout the year, nearly half are members of religious orders. Virginity features more prominently among women than men; the threat of loss of virginity is often a key point of crisis. St Winifred, for example, seventh-century Welsh abbess whose feast day is 3 November, was beheaded while trying to protect her chastity. Several other figures are named as mothers of saints; no similar father figure is so named. Women, then, are harder to come by in the lectionary, and those that do occur are often either featured because of their relationship to a male relative, or are celibate by calling. In both cases, ordinary modern women might find these figures and their lifestyles somewhat two-dimensional or rather distant and not easy to identify with.

In my search for women to include in my sermon series, I decided to range both within and beyond the lectionary to find figures that would be relevant and challenging to my largely female congregation. I included from the calendar Manche Masemola, a young twentieth-century African martyr killed by her people for refusing to give up her new-found faith; and Maude Royden, English suffragist, lecturer and world-travelled preacher, the first female Doctor of Divinity and campaigner for women's ordination in the 1930s. My list also featured Etty Hillesum, a young Dutch Jewish woman whose diaries of life through the Second World War reveal an extraordinary spiritual journey and search for meaning. Then there is Edwina Gateley, a contemporary British-born mystic, theologian and poet, whose call has led her from being among Maasai women of East Africa to befriending street girls in Chicago; and Joyce Rupp, a North American sister whose accessible spiritual writings have inspired people across the globe and are widely available.

My project led me to search beyond the more obvious sources to find material appropriate to women's experience and needs.

This is also the case when studying Scripture in preparation for a sermon. Parishes that use the lectionary have manageable portions of Scripture carefully selected for each day of the year. The lectionary readings are heard and read by the worshipping congregation and those who preach, as well as by scholars, theologians, hymn writers and all those reading Scripture for private devotion. Those who hear Scripture being read and preached Sunday by Sunday are often largely women, but those who have interpreted Scripture and selected texts have overwhelmingly been men.

Among biblical figures, women's presence is often ignored or underplayed by the writers of Scripture (possibly all men). Their stories are recorded and interpreted by male writers and teachers from a masculine point of view so that their own feminine perspective is obscured. We are told in the Gospel of Matthew, for instance, that Jesus fed five thousand men – the number of women and children was not recorded (Matt. 14.13). Again, we hear that Jesus said of the woman who anointed him with costly ointment, 'what she has done will be told in remembrance of her' (Matt. 26.13); but the author gives us no name to remember her by.

Where we meet them at all, women in Scripture often carry negative connotations. Eve, the first mother, gave in to temptation and so was held responsible for suffering and sin. The people of God in the Old Testament and the Church in the New Testament are often depicted in terms of wife and bride. But these female figures have often been redeemed from a state of sin, whoredom and defilement. The image of the adulterous wife was often used for the unfaithfulness of God's chosen people. Ezekiel, for example, rails against Israel's faithlessness, comparing it with the uncleanness of a woman's menstrual blood (Ezek. 36.17). (It is interesting to note that *The Message*, a modern version of the Bible in contemporary language, de-genders this allusion to impurity in its translation 'the polluted blood they poured out on the ground'. Compare this with the King James Version, 'their way was before me as the uncleanness of a removed woman').

The Church is the redeemed bride, a once reviled object of impurity, rescued by Christ the bridegroom from defilement. In the past, theologians taught that the female body was a source of sexual temptation and sin, a distraction from the holy. A woman's femaleness was linked with shame and had to be veiled and kept under control, especially in church. Natural functions associated with femininity, including childbirth and menstruation, were seen as ritually unclean and so were subject to taboos and regulations.

Preaching with women in mind

Preachers who are aware of this imbalance have the opportunity to search for woman's hidden voice in Scripture and to offer an interpretation that speaks into the experiences and desires of both the women and the men in their congregations. The sensitive preacher will also be alert to the social and historical context of any biblical text, and will be wary of any interpretation that might perpetuate male T-for-G, such as unnuanced notions of woman as either unattainably saintlike, unutterably sinful or valued solely as wife and mother.

Opportunities will arise to make use of feminine as well as masculine metaphors for God. We have to look harder in Scripture for these, because there are far fewer of them, and those that exist have been rather overlooked by the male T-for-G of our religious culture. In *A Theology of Women's Priesthood* I list a number of these maternal metaphors, which associate God with the female reproductive cycle (the womb, pregnancy, childbirth) and with childcare (2009:52–60). These reflect the caring, creative God who labours to bring forth and nurture new life. Yahweh, for instance, is depicted as midwife to the nation (Isa. 66.7–9), while Jesus, yearning to embrace Jerusalem, identifies himself with the humble hen protecting her young (Matt. 23.37).

Feminist biblical criticism is a well-established discipline, and any serious biblical study now pays attention to the role (or indeed the absence) of women in biblical texts, their place in contemporary society at the time Scripture was written and the way women are regarded (if at all) by the author. Preachers who are aware of sexual difference will similarly pay attention to these themes as they read, interpret and talk with others about Scripture in the course of their sermon preparation. As Carol Newsom and Sharon Ringe point out in their Introduction to *Women's Bible Commentary*, 'There is a great sense of empowerment . . . that comes from reading the Bible as a woman in the company of other women.'

Preachers and priests who are sensitive to issues of gender can apply their understanding in relating Scripture to contemporary culture and everyday ministry. Bishop David, speaking from his South African context, told me that he recognizes how much the Church colludes with 'the huge patriarchal discourse of society. We need to re-construct it – look at abuse in terms of HIV, AIDS, rape as a power issue, the idea of what it means to be a man.' These are the sorts of pressing social issues, all gender-related, that can be approached through a careful, gender-aware reading of Scripture.

Sometimes, in preaching, this might be a matter simply of bringing to notice the women in the story. The midwives Puah and Shiphrah were instrumental in the story of Moses' early life (Exod. 1.15), but I have never heard them mentioned from the pulpit. I recently began a sermon by mentioning their names; no one in the congregation could identify them. Yet their courageous, prophetic disobedience to Pharaoh – what we might today call a form of non-violent direct action – helped the Hebrews to survive. The fact that, unusually, the writer records their names in Scripture allows the opportunity for them to be mentioned by name and more readily remembered.

On occasions it can be fruitful to reflect on women's experience so as to render an interpretation of Scripture that is different from those offered by older commentaries. Stories around the death and resurrection of Jesus provide opportunities here, since women are prominent in the story, not least because at certain points in the narrative the authors of the Gospels had only women's first-hand testimony to go by. Several contemporary women authors have adopted an imaginative, poetic approach to interpretation of Scripture in their exploration of the women in Jesus' life. In *Soul Sisters* (2005), Edwina Gateley, together with artist Louis Glanzman, compellingly depicts a dozen women from the New Testament, with a view to making Scripture speak afresh to readers today. Tina Beattie, in *The Last Supper according to Martha and Mary* (2001), similarly offers a lyrical and dramatic account of two familiar characters who were followers of Jesus. Margaret Hebblethwaite's *Six New Gospels* (1994) gives accounts through the life of Christ from the viewpoint of six women close to Jesus. All these publications are both scholarly and at the same time passionate and poetic, and they provide much food for the thoughtful preacher who seeks to read beyond the conventions of traditional hermeneutics.

Many passages in the Old Testament present particular challenges to the gender-aware preacher. Hosea's treatment of Gomer is conventionally interpreted in the context of the boundless love of a husband towards an unfaithful wife, the story being a metaphor for Yahweh's love for Israel despite the nation's disobedience. But an interpretation sensitive to the lack of marital rights afforded to many wives worldwide and to the sexual exploitation and domestic abuse suffered by many women raises some awkward questions. What is the nature of a marriage that allows a woman to be treated as property, and for whom the punishment meted out by her husband is to be sexually abused by several men? These texts do not make for an easy task for the gender-aware preacher; they cannot be treated *only* as metaphors that can in any straightforward way be mapped onto today's consciousness.

In the past few years a number of writers have published material that confronts the difficulties presented by texts written in the context of male T-for-G. Phyllis Trible, for example, in *Texts of Terror* (1984) reinterprets the tragic and neglected stories of four Old Testament women and poses challenging questions about misogyny in Scripture and in traditional hermeneutics. In *Women's Bible Commentary* (Newsom and Ringe 1998) a group of female academics summarize and comment on Scripture that has particular relevance to women – a valuable resource for preachers. Athalya Brenner has published several volumes of scholarly feminist writing about biblical texts. These are all serious biblical studies that provide helpful material for those who take both preaching and sexual difference seriously. They can assist a preacher looking for women's presence to notice what is absent, and weave a woman's voice among the gaps in the text.

In the book of Genesis, for instance, we are told that Jacob's daughter Dinah is raped by Shechem, but she is given no personality of her own in the text; we never hear her voice or her side of the story at any time. She was let down by her family and by the culture of her time. But the writer does not let us know what Dinah herself feels or says about her plight or her pain. Dinah and several other female figures in the Old Testament are linked with male violence or abuse or are treated as the property of men. This story prompts a reflection on the enforced silence of victims of sexual abuse or other injustices sustained by those on the margins of society; and on the inner freedom that comes often after great suffering, a freedom that need not be crippled by past events.

Susan Durber has been concerned about a general disillusionment with preaching, and the lack of recent reflection on its potential power to transform faith. In *Preaching Like a Woman* (2007) she notes that many women do not enjoy preaching, and that some see it as a more appropriate ministry for men. I have come across this attitude myself. A female colleague recently told me that she thought women don't preach as well as men. She offered no explanation for her essentialist belief that femaleness somehow disabled one's preaching faculties. Durber seeks to reaffirm the role of preaching as a primary place for shaping and defining faith. She argues that this must include making the Church a place of true welcome, hospitality and life for women. To this end, she offers some down-to-earth guidance in interpreting Scripture from a feminist perspective while developing an effective preaching voice from one's own life, faith and experience. She includes suggestions on ways of interpreting texts from Old and New Testaments and throughout the Christian year. To preach 'like a woman', she maintains, is about:

> Bringing to voice what has been silenced in the Church, to offer both a challenge to the patriarchal traditions in which Christianity has been embedded and a remaking of the faith in more inclusive and transforming speech. Women need to 'come out' and to find spaces where they may speak for the God who created women and men in God's image and the God who is creating a new humanity.   (2007:12)

Deborah, in her preaching, has sought and found those spaces in her ministry. She grew up a Methodist in a conservative part of the USA, where male-dominated language and interpretation of Scripture were the norm. 'But I have always found that I apply a feminist hermeneutic quite naturally, because that is what I am – a woman. I don't try to ram it down people's throats, but it is my perspective.' She remembers, in a church in London in 1990, being given 'the New Man' as the text for her sermon. 'This careless language was difficult for me – especially when I noticed that in the congregation was Janet Morley' (Morley had recently published the first edition of *All Desires Known*, which became a well-loved collection of prayers using inclusive language).

Preaching like a woman means not only looking for women's voice in Scripture and tradition, but also naming women's experience as a valid and valuable part of the ongoing narrative of faith. Rebecca, in her mixed-sex clergy team in England, found that there was a conscious effort to 'bring all human experience, bodily included, into the pulpit'. She recalled one incident when the team specifically wanted to make use of her bodily experience:

> They agreed that on the Advent Sunday following the Christmas when my first child was born, it *had* to be me who preached at a service (devised by a new grandfather who was part of the wider

team at that church) which was to be on the theme 'Waiting to be born'. They said, 'Well, you're the only member of the team who's given birth – you *have* to preach!'

To speak, as Rebecca did, from the point of view not only of a priest but also as a mother, a birth-giving woman, a sexual being, has strong symbolic resonances that are at once power-fully evocative and destabilizing to traditional taboos and beliefs. When as women we bring our own bodiliness into the ministry of the word, we are affirming that our bodies are as much a focus for the presence of God as are those of men. We are opening up a sacred space that is available to both women and men, because all women experience female bodiliness and all of us, male and female, have been born of women and know that a mother's womb nurtured our earliest life.

Speaking with a woman's voice can also open up a space for others who have been marginalized, ignored and disempowered. When the voiceless come to speech, desire can be translated from rhetoric to commitment and action. Joanna joined a parish with several male priests:

> I found myself positively encouraged by male – and largely gay – colleagues, to bring the experience of married woman, and mother, to my preaching and to our other work. On one occasion, heavily pregnant, I accompanied a male priest to a church meeting. He had been persecuted by local church leaders for his pro-gay stance, and he had agreed to attend the meeting to answer questions about his being gay. I remember it as a very uncomfortable encounter. I made very little contribution beyond my presence, but the attempt to 'normalize' the situation did not go unnoticed by either party. Here in Central London the alliance between ordained women and gay male clergy is noteworthy perhaps. I suppose we have common cause re the institutional church, but it goes more deeply than that I think.

A feminist hermeneutic of 'reading between the lines' can be applied beyond the boundaries of sex and gender to other differences and other silences, for instance of age, ability and race. June, ministering in a parish in London, says:

I definitely do apply a feminist hermeneutic, but I tend to find that it leads me beyond women's experience to look for other lost voices too – especially those who are nameless or whose stories break off in the middle. The Ethiopian eunuch in Acts, for example – whatever happened to him when he went back to Candace's court? I want to know!

There is no gender bar on applying this kind of hermeneutic to Scripture; preachers of both sexes can be attentive to the voice of what is left unspoken and unrecorded, in order to interpret the still small voice of God. But where both women and men share the pulpit, and where those preachers are responsive to differences in people's ways of being and knowing, then they are more able to speak into the hearts and minds of the whole church family in all its diversity.

Prayer book language

On my bookshelves is *A New Zealand Prayer Book*, titled in Maori *He Karakia Mihinare o Aotearoa*, first published in 1989. The language of the prayers is simple, direct and dignified. I particularly like the Benedicite Aotearoa, a form of the Song of Creation, which is both inclusive of ethnicity and gender, and specific in naming indigenous and introduced creatures of the islands:

> Rabbits and cattle, moths and dogs,
> kiwi and sparrow and tui and hawk:
> give to our God your thanks and praise.
>
> You Maori and Pakeha, women and men,
> all who inhabit the long white cloud:
> give to our God your thanks and praise.
> From *A New Zealand Prayer Book*. © Used by permission.

The Thanksgiving for the Gift of a Child (no mention of 'Churching' here) is designed to take place not necessarily in church, as directed by the Book of Common Prayer, but perhaps in hospital or at home, or any suitable setting convenient for the family. Again, it departs from the traditional thanksgiving in specifically mentioning its intended use for adoptive as well 'birth' children, and by being led by a deacon or authorized layperson rather than necessarily by a priest.

In *A New Zealand Prayer Book*, the prayer for the mother after delivery of her child, in giving thanks for bringing her safely through pregnancy and labour, differs from the traditional words by naming her as one who has been called to share in God's creative acts, and praying 'in the name of him who was born of a woman'. There are also prayers to be said by the natural parents of an adopted child, by the mother, father, adoptive parents and other family members. A prayer for the family and home names God as Earth-maker, Pain-bearer, Lifegiver, Father and Mother. These simple but profound changes have brought to acknowledgement the daughters of God and the mystery of the Incarnation through the God-given procreative powers of a human mother. They all serve as an example of prayer that pays attention to people's real lives, and affirms the link between everyday human experiences, including those of women, and the active presence of God in them.

The Introduction to *A New Zealand Prayer Book* makes mention of the great changes that have taken place in New Zealand over the previous quarter century, including a growing ecological awareness, and the adoption of the Maori tongue as an official language of the nation. Other developments mentioned include the ordination of women, which has 'ensured a continuing dialogue on the equal partnership of women and men within the Church' and an 'increasing need to choose language which is inclusive in nature and which affirms the place of each gender under God' (1989:x). Mention is made of the desire to close the gap between liturgical language and the words common to everyday life. In order to enable the worshipping community to pray, there is a quest to find 'ways to address God in language which is other than masculine and triumphal' (1989:xii).

It is no accident that the inclusive outlook of this prayer book has coincided with a commitment at all levels to women's ordained ministry. Within a few years of the approval of women's ordination, Auckland had female staff training ordinands and in the year the *Prayer Book* was published, Dunedin had the first female diocesan bishop in the Anglican Communion. The use of inclusive language is just one of a raft of ways that the province of New Zealand/Aotearoa is seeking to establish and affirm equality and partnership between the sexes and within a mix of cultures.

Dorothy, speaking to me in Napier, said, 'The Church has made a commitment from the top down to adopt inclusive language. We always use gender-neutral language in referring to each other in liturgy. We're fortunate in this province – it's the norm.' Meredith, also in Napier, commented, 'There was a real push for inclusive liturgies in the 1990s – those in favour just used it and congregations became familiar with it.' Ros, an associate priest, told me that she and her male vicar were always very careful about God-language, and would avoid using the male pronoun for God in preaching or in conversation.

Jean told me about a sister in a community in Auckland who questioned the necessity for inclusive language:

> She would say 'Why bother with it?' Then she went on leave to England, where she had been born, and when she returned she told us she had never realized how sexist God-talk was back at home. She had been immersed for four years in a religious community that had consciously adopted gender-neutral language – as was true for the Church and for wider society in New Zealand. In that time her own perspective had shifted.

In England and Wales, at a parish level, the use of gender-neutral language has been more haphazard than systematic. The language of *Common Worship* uses gender-neutral terms for human beings and has reduced the use of male pronouns in relation to God. It has also adopted a more generally inclusive approach in its pastoral services. The Thanksgiving for the Gift of a Child, for instance, includes prayers for the father, grandparents and siblings and also for health workers, adoptive parents and children with special needs. But there is no prayer specifically for the mother, nor any mention of her part in the prenatal life or the birth of her child. In the current edition of the Episcopal Church's Book of Common Prayer (it has had its own version since the American Revolution) allowance is made in the thanksgiving prayers for the birth or adoption of a child for parents to express thanks in their own words.

Alice, a vicar in the Highveld, acknowledges the need for inclusive language, which she reports has not yet become the norm in South Africa:

> They increasingly use terms such as 'Mothering God' alongside the more traditional male imagery – but never completely in place of them. I have found myself using inclusive language to refer to God in sermons, often using more neutral terms [and] not using male pronouns, but rather speaking of Nurturing God, Loving God or God, who is our Mother and Father. This is greatly assisted in the Black African culture where personal pronouns for male or female do not exist – although God is most often viewed in male terms through tribal societal culture and entrenched in English biblical and missionary inculturation.

Alice runs programmes of Spiritual Formation. 'It is in these spaces', she says, 'that I feel most free to grapple with feminist imagery of God, and the roles of male and female.' Here she finds she can engage her parishioners, male and female, to discuss what she calls 'equalitarian living', listening to the woman's voice in Scripture, and 'encouraging both men and women to engage in reflection on their own lives, and how they have been "conditioned" into present attitudes and paradigms'.

Congregational worship

Jessica, a senior clergywoman in a Welsh diocese, commented that there are difficulties in trying to hurry the pace of modifying language where congregations aren't ready. 'Inclusive language can't be forced on a congregation – that's counter-productive.' A congregation that is fond of its traditional language may be resistant to change. Equally, a church that is committed to hospitality, to mission and evangelism, will want to use language that expands people's understanding of God and reflects the gospel message that all human beings are loved by God. Church is the place where people come to find acceptance at their deepest level of being. Words used in worship can hurt as well as heal, oppress as well as liberate, and those who are used to inclusive language in the world beyond the church threshold are likely to feel rejected when the language inside excludes them. Patrick, a priest who has ministered both in Wales and England, said:

> Being married to a woman priest has made me far more sensitive to the power of language to diminish and exclude, not that I was previously unaware. It became a matter of much more importance to avoid male gendered language in the liturgy, in Bible translations and in hymns. I have started to refer to the Trinity as Creator, Saviour and Comforter. I'm not quite used to that one yet though. But I'm getting there.

An English prison chaplain, Julie, told me that working in an all-female environment made her particularly sensitive to use of language. 'At the weekly non-eucharistic service on Sunday afternoons I read from the psalms, and change the language to make it more inclusive for the women listening.'

Dawn, in New Zealand, commented, 'I always use inclusive language except for hymns at services at Christmas, or funerals, when I get out the old traditional hymns familiar to those who don't attend church regularly.' Hymnology is one area of worship where women remain largely invisible. Women have been writing hymns for generations, and make up the majority of those who sing them. Excluded from many forms of ministry and from leadership in church worship, women have long expressed and influenced spiritual understanding in the less rigidly controlled form of hymnology. However, there has been a dearth of female biblical figures and women's experience among our favourite songs of worship.

I recently gave a talk at a Methodist women's group. The meeting began with the hymn 'I am the bread of life' written by S. Suzanne Toolan in 1966. Throughout the five verses, all of the exclusively female group enthusiastically sang about the man who responds to Christ – 'he who comes to me', 'he who believes in me', 'he shall live forever', and so on. I found this non-inclusive language distanced me uncomfortably from the personal message of salvation that the words were intended to convey. I wondered why all we women were not making the hymn our own simply by applying a more appropriate personal pronoun. Perhaps when words get printed in black and white they take on an immutability that resists adaptation (in fact an inclusive version is printed in *Complete Anglican Hymns Old & New*, 2000). Amy, in her New Zealand parish, found this problem and tackled the matter herself. 'Hymns are still a problem. The language of hymns hasn't changed. In my parish I changed the words of all hymns, old and new, to make them gender-neutral.'

On the whole, writers of newer hymns and prayers and compilers of newer ritual are aware of the need to redress the marginalization of women in the context of liturgy. The Church has always struggled with gender issues, in acts of worship as in other areas of ministry; and this problem is starting to be addressed as more women are themselves becoming authoritative agents of change as scholars, priests, theologians and liturgists. Teresa Berger, Roman Catholic theologian and liturgical scholar, notes that 'The problem for many women . . . is not that liturgy is meaningless; the problem comes with the kind of liturgies to which women are invited' (1999:148–9). Many liturgies, she believes from her experience in Europe and North America, lack relevance for women's lives and experience today. Women are symbol-makers and shapers of narrative and tradition, and these charisms need to be cherished by the worshipping community as part of the wider movement of liturgical renewal. It is counter-productive to the gospel, in Berger's view, for worship to remain a space where 'gender relations are still those of past dominations and marginalizations' (1999:153).

Janet Walton, an American scholar in liturgy, lists in *Feminist Liturgy* (1999) some practical examples of how recognition of women's perspectives and world-view might affect worship. These might well be simple matters to do with women's general preference for non-hierarchical relationships and structures. Such a preference might be expressed by the arrangement of chairs in the round so that everyone can see and hear each other easily, and so that no one person, even the leader, is placed 'above' another. She mentions the making of horizontal gestures that affirm equality and interdependence, and the use of a range of musical instruments, songs and movements so as to echo the principle of inclusion. Janet Wootton, an English Congregationalist minister, makes similar observations about worship space and shape in *Introducing a Practical Feminist Theology of Worship*. She notes that altars have moved nearer to the people, preachers often eschew the pulpit and address the congregation at eye-level, and acts of worship are often arranged in the round (2000:55).

Liturgical developments such as these have come from rethinking traditional patterns shaped by male T-for-G where, typically, a privileged man (probably white and middle class) took charge and most others (including all women) barely had a voice. Increasing numbers of women in ordained ministry have coincided with much liturgical renewal developing from and for a variety of pastoral needs. This may be in part because laypeople see female ministers as more approachable and less authoritarian; they don't carry the weight of symbolism associated with cultural power as men do. Women may also be affirmed by a minister of their own sex and feel that they can share problems with someone who can draw on their own similar experiences.

The last few decades have seen many experiments in using symbols, choreography and words to express worshippers' relationship with God, with each other and with the created world in ways that are more authentic and relevant for today's worshippers. Much liturgical renewal has sought to honour distinctions in human experience, and reflect them in worship, on the understanding that to ignore aspects of human understanding and aspiration is also to limit our relationship with God.

Pastoral care and special services

Where those in pastoral ministry pay attention to sexual difference, then they may want to develop prayers and liturgies that meet needs and mark occasions, often associated with life-cycle events, which have historically been overlooked. All Souls' Day, for example, can be a time for remembering stillborn or miscarried babies, who were barely acknowledged in the past. Even if those babies were never named, a mention of them at a time of commemoration can bring healing to parents who perhaps were never given the opportunity to properly grieve at the time of their loss.

Rituals may be needed for survivors of domestic or sexual abuse, whether male or female, where there are likely to be issues around anger, healing, victimhood, justice and forgiveness. A prison chaplain told me of one female inmate who wanted to light a candle and say a prayer in chapel for her brother on the anniversary of his death. The chaplain suspected a conflicting mass of emotions, and possibly a history of abuse, when the prisoner asked her, 'Am I very bad if I can't forgive somebody?' Some needs – especially where issues affecting the body and sexuality are concerned – are more appropriately dealt with by a minister of the same sex; and where male and female clergy are ministering together, then discernment can be used about who should lead ritual intended to address specific pastoral situations.

Patrick has many years of experience as a chaplain in male prisons, and now ministers for a few hours a week in a female prison in England. He told me about two women prisoners who came to him for a rite of reconciliation. For most pastoral and personal matters, Patrick knew they would certainly go to the full-time, ordained female chaplain. She was the familiar face, and they trusted her at a personal level. 'But these two came to me for sacramental confession.' Patrick offered two possible explanations, not mutually exclusive:

One is that men in black clerical shirts are the ones who hear confessions – a sort of religious folk memory perhaps. The other

71

possibility is that it was precisely because I was less familiar, more distant. As another prisoner once put it to me, 'I'm only telling you all this because you don't matter.' This wasn't rudeness but an acknowledgement I wouldn't tell other people in the prison and that we wouldn't meet again after one of us moved on.

Attention to difference is important not only in pastoral needs as they arise, but also in the worship of the community week by week, as it responds to the breadth of human experience and desire. Take Mothering Sunday, for example, when the custom is to give thanks for our mothers and remember Mother Church – and often to give posies to mothers in the congregation. It's usually a time for a little leavening of the Lenten period, when the church remains otherwise undecorated with flowers. But actually, motherhood is a pretty complicated business, not always associated with joy and thankfulness; for some it can be about loss, sadness, guilt, resentment.

This came home to me especially strongly when I was a chaplain in a male lifer prison. For many of the inmates, the idea of motherhood was connected with painful emotions and memories. Some men came from dysfunctional, abusive or broken homes; complex feelings toward their own mothers were often dealt with by denial, grief, anger or anxiety. I met some men who could barely talk about their mothers without showing distress, and others who told me they would gladly kill their mothers given a chance. I wanted to take account of this gamut of emotional responses in a service that would be meaningful and relevant to that congregation, and honest about their feelings in the context of worship.

For the eucharistic service that emerged, I arranged the chairs in a horseshoe shape around the altar. The liturgy included pieces written and read by three of the inmates, and reflected their own differing experiences of their mothers. I passed around a basket of stones, inviting everyone to choose one and regard it as a symbol of how they were feeling at that moment about their own mothers – loss, bereavement, tenderness, hurt and so on. I reminded them that whatever our feelings were, God knew about them already and was waiting for us to offer them up with honesty and openness. The stones were put on the altar, and confession and absolution followed, incorporating words to reflect the range of feelings expressed. In the talk (more of a dialogue with the men rather than a sermon) I included maternal images of God and led a reflection on how we can aspire towards the self-giving love God shows towards us.

There are several reasons, I think, why the form of this service could be attributed to the type of renewal in liturgy developed by scholars working from a feminist perspective. For one thing, the worship was planned collaboratively with several men who offered their thoughts and who wrote and read out their own stories. We all listened and learnt from each other; there was no single, hierarchical line of authority. The liturgy did not impose a definitive viewpoint, but generated a spectrum of feelings and responses, some quite uncomfortable. All were encouraged to own their particular experiences and to speak for themselves. This mix of responses was offered to God with the expectation of blessing. Solidarity, inclusion and equality were reinforced physically by the arrangement of the worship space. Time and space were given for the unexpected response, for the unpredicted question, for the possibility that transformation and healing might begin. God was named both as father and mother, allowing for the complexity of the human parent–child bond that colours our relationship with God. The vast range of emotions and responses that I tried to encompass and address in that service are not dissimilar to those experienced week by week in every parish, which may well be present (although unacknowledged) at emotive occasions such as Mothering Sunday.

Where God is referred to only in male terms, problems can arise for both women and men who have experienced difficult or abusive relationships with their own father. Gender-neutral language, or the occasional naming of God in feminine terms, can help to expand our notion of God and to respond to God's presence in ways that are refreshing, appropriate and fruitful. In *A Theology of Women's Priesthood*, I look at maternal divine images for God in Scripture through the perspective of the human reproductive cycle – the womb, the menses, labour, childbirth, suckling, nurturing, caring, letting go (2009:52–9). There is a treasure-house of such images to be explored for those who want to reach beyond a church tradition that has long been dominated by male images. Suffice it to say here that, where flexibility is allowed, the language of worship can be tailored to the needs and desires of particular congregations, times and seasons, and can open up new horizons in exploring our relationship with God and with each other.

They struggled beside me

When Paul, on one of his missionary journeys, arrives at the great Roman colony of Philippi in Macedonia, a few miles north of the Aegean Sea, he finds no synagogue. He and his three companions join the worshippers who are meeting for prayer by the river, outside the city gate. Most of this group are women, and some are Gentile 'godfearers' attracted to the Jewish religion. Among them is Lydia, a wealthy businesswoman from Thyatira who deals in costly purple goods. In Hellenistic times, women in Macedonia probably enjoyed greater freedom than in other Mediterranean lands, and so were able, like Lydia, actively to participate in social and economic life.

When Lydia hears Paul talk, Luke records that 'The Lord opened her heart' (Acts 16.14). What did she hear God saying to her through Paul? What did she find in Paul's message that was so compelling? Tantalizingly, Luke doesn't tell us. But we can be sure that this Gentile made a free choice; she wasn't simply following the lead of a husband or master. Something about this New Way appealed to her, spoke to her life experience and desire. Perhaps Paul was underlining the point that the good news wasn't just for the few, but for everyone – Jew and Gentile, male and female, slave and free – who has ears to hear and a heart to respond. So it was that she became Paul's first convert in Europe and was baptized in the river, as were her household.

One of Lydia's first responses, realizing that Paul and his fellow missionaries need a base, is to offer them hospitality in her own home. So this woman of means thus plays a crucial role in the formation of the early Church in Europe. The first believers gathered together for prayer and worship in private households, where leadership and liturgy evolved and adapted to local need and custom. Such gatherings were often hosted by the woman of the house. In Lydia's case, the initial community would have been her family, servants and perhaps employees. Thus her domain became the nucleus of one of the earliest Christian communities.

In responding to and co-operating with Paul, Lydia and other women played a pivotal part in bringing the gospel to their own locality. Paul recognized their calling, their gifts and their leadership as instrumental in his apostolic ministry. With his active support and encouragement, women ministered as hosts of church gatherings, teachers and exemplars of good works. Two of its very active and probably foundational members were Euodia and Syntyche, mentioned by Paul in his letter to the Philippians (4.2–3). He urges the congregation to help these women, 'for they struggled beside me in the work of the gospel' (Phil. 4.3). Here is an indication of the very active and influential part women played as co-workers alongside their male counterparts.

We cannot know for certain exactly what role women played in the formation of the early Church, in its worship, pastoral ministry, outreach and so on. But Luke and Paul provide us with a picture of a community of faith where women and men ministered side by side as co-workers. There was the missionary couple Prisca and Aquila (Rom. 16.3) who worked alongside Paul and risked their lives; Junia was a prominent apostle (Rom. 16.7), imprisoned with Andronicus and Paul (Rom. 16.7); Phoebe is described as a sister, *diakonos* (deacon) and *prostates* (patron) (Rom. 16.1–2).

Paul describes the Church community in terms of the body of Christ (Romans 12; 1 Cor. 12; Eph. 4), where each member, inspired by the Spirit, exercises his or her gifts in ministry. He gives us a picture of a community of mutual interdependence, showing a reversal of the usual ideas about status and importance that held sway in the wider culture of male T-for-G. Here a new way was being forged, built on the foundations of love, equality and unity. We see the outworking of this belief in Christian baptism, open to women and men, boys and girls, which took over as the distinctive mark of belonging from circumcision, the Jewish male-only equivalent. From now on, as Paul says, all people are equal before God and, in relation to redemption and spiritual gifts, all have equal standing (Gal. 3.28). Since those early days, there have been countless Lydias who have built up the Church with their gifts and experience, their leadership skills and acumen.

Women and men today in a priesthood of both sexes affirm that the female body, as much as the male, is made in the image of God and is an equally powerful signifier of the sacred. Together, they can find again the lost and ignored voice of women and their experience in history, in Scripture, in worship, in pastoral ministry. Then, working as equal partners in ministry, women and men can embody the wholeness of the Church, the body of Christ.

4

Being and working together

Bringing us to harmony

Not long ago I found myself sitting in a party leader's chair in the Scottish Parliament in Edinburgh. I was being shown around the new building by a Member, and was impressed by the shape of the debating chamber. Designed in a hemicycle, or horseshoe shape, it is intended to encourage consensus rather than confrontation among political factions. The Welsh National Assembly building in Cardiff, opened two years later in 2006, has a broadly similar debating chamber in a circular configuration. What a contrast to the older chamber at Westminster, designed so that government and opposition parties confront each other on opposing sets of benches. It was fascinating to see how the English building coped with the new politics ushered in by the 2010 general election, which resulted in a hung parliament. Since no one party gained an overall majority of seats, the Conservative and Liberal Democrat parties struck a deal to share power in the first full coalition since the end of World War II.

Coalitions are a pretty common form of government elsewhere – voters in India, Finland or Israel would probably hardly raise an eyebrow – but it was a major change for the UK. The result was an intriguing spectacle of members from the main Conservative party being joined on the government benches by some Liberal Democrat ministers, and trying to work together in a more consensual way for which the chamber wasn't originally intended.

The new Scottish and Welsh buildings reflect a shift in our society towards a more consensual, accountable and transparent form of working that permeates many areas of contemporary public and private life. It closely correlates with an

increasingly inclusive attitude towards those previously overlooked or discriminated against because of race, age, disability,
sex or some other difference. The norms of middle-class, white
male T-for-G, with its particular ways of thinking, relating and
behaving – whatever shape they take in any given culture – are
now being challenged. In today's workplace, and in our homes,
we may well be looking for co-operation as well as competition,
collaboration rather than domination, equality as much as hierarchy. Marriage for many couples no longer means a family
organized as a male head of the household who rules in varying degrees over his wife, children and servants. Politics – as
we are finding out in the UK – does not have to be conducted
like tilting knights in a medieval jousting match.

The novel shift at Westminster reflects similar changes in
Church life. Throughout the Anglican Communion, and other
denominations, there has been a move over the last generation
towards a more collaborative approach to ministry. The focus
has moved from individual competence and authority towards
mutual responsibility and interdependence within a community that seeks to release and harness the gifts of all. Priestly
leadership in a parish or group of parishes is now often not
held by one individual but shared across a team of people, both
ordained and lay, each contributing their own experiences and
talents. These working groups present their own challenges and
opportunities, including the ability and willingness of members
to work effectively in collaboration with others. These are
qualities now sought and expected in prospective ordinands.
The selection criteria for the Church in Wales, for instance, ask
for the capacity 'to collaborate effectively with others', for a
'commitment to collaboration in team working', and for 'group
work skills'.

In his first letter to the Corinthians, Paul tells the community of believers that when they gather for worship, each should
be prepared, as *The Message* translation puts it, with 'something
that will be useful for all' (1 Cor. 14.26). When someone speaks,
others should listen to what is said and take it to heart. Every
person should take his or her turn, with no one person taking

over; all should learn from each other. 'When we worship the right way', he adds, 'God doesn't stir us up into confusion; he brings us into harmony' (1 Cor. 14.33). I think these words of advice about worship are equally valid for the way we best work collaboratively together in order to further God's Kingdom. We are called to live and work together as members of Christ's body, equal under God, and at the same time to be distinct and unique individuals, with our own complementary, mutually enriching and diverse qualities and talents.

This model of ordained ministry relies on more interdependent, mutually accountable working practices, and a willingness to share authority and decision-making. It involves a style of teamwork that is concerned with identifying and releasing the gifts of all of its members so that everyone can participate and reach his or her full potential. Collaborative ministry has no single, distinct definition, but it involves less hierarchical structures and methods, a less dictatorial style of leadership and a greater sense of equality. A good team is committed to resolving problems and overcoming barriers to good working relations as they occur. Chosen working methods allow each member of the team to feel empowered, included and encouraged, and to make a valid contribution to a common purpose. A good team member brings out the best in others and is sensitive to others' distinct personal world-view and preferred working styles. To be effective, members of the group need to be aware of their own foibles, prejudices and weaknesses, and be willing to share power. The various gifts that each member brings are recognized and nurtured, and each person is committed to a shared vision.

Working collaboratively with others is never a simple matter. Whether it's getting the children to tidy their rooms, or negotiating a household task with our partner, or planning a church service or parish project, there's often the thought that 'I could do this quicker and better by myself'. Working together in a team is not always the speediest option, and there are many pitfalls to be overcome. People may not subscribe to a shared vision and language, or be able to agree working methods, or feel comfortable with leadership styles and accountability. Where these elements fall down, the result can be a collaborative inertia which prevents or slows down the community reaching their hoped-for goal. Difficulties may arise because an individual harbours unwarranted presuppositions about how things ought to be done. Another may be dissatisfied with a perceived imbalance in power or status.

In the church community, collaborative styles of leadership are still a relatively new phenomenon, so they can be counter-cultural in the sense that they run against the grain of so many traditional structures and practices. Those who have in the past held a sole position of power and responsibility have to be willing to accept differing points of view and others' priorities and preferences. They must be careful not to expect their own viewpoint to dominate, or to always get their own way. They have to be willing to change old patterns of thinking and behaviour, and to be open to others' experiences and judgements. An individual or group may appear to assent to the theology of collaborative ministry, but in practice the preferred ways of working may still be hierarchical and autocratic, causing tensions and lowering morale among colleagues who are committed to more collaborative practices.

Working with sexual difference

Nathan trained as a priest in Brisbane. Some years later his ministry took him and his family to southern Brazil. Among his new colleagues was Rosa, a young deacon. Nathan found that his theological training had been similar to Rosa's and had equipped him to minister effectively alongside her:

> Australia had embraced feminism much more than Brazil had and I was also married to someone who had strong feminist views. I think my theological training in an era of reflection on liberation theology and when issues of women's ordination were very much on the agenda formed my own views and beliefs.

Another colleague was Paulo, who earned his living as a mechanic. Nathan felt that Paulo had been ordained when it was 'fashionable among Anglican bishops to romanticize the worker priest who had had Theological Education by Extension. Certainly he had never been given the opportunity to study theology at a seminary.'

The bishop envisaged that Nathan, Rosa and Paulo would work collaboratively in a small Anglican community. The first obstacle came very early on:

> Paulo had no desire to work in a team. Perhaps he felt threatened by a foreigner or by the woman who would soon be ordained as a priest. Both of us had more theological training which could be described as liberal and possible leftist. The simple solution was to divide the area. Rosa and I would look after half, and Paulo the other half. It is hard to tell how much the division was driven by the woman factor or the foreigner factor or the theological factors.

Nathan relied heavily on Rosa since he was still learning Portuguese. Rosa, in her turn, had to rely on Nathan at first since she could not celebrate the Eucharist:

> Perhaps because of our mutual needs and similar theological views we developed a good friendship. We had different personalities and different strengths and weaknesses. On the whole we were able to complement each other and formed a strong partnership. As I grew in my skills of communication in Portuguese and Rosa was ordained we continued to work closely together, sharing preaching and worship leadership. We prepared teaching material together. Rosa corrected or rewrote some of my material to make it more understandable. She contributed her own work which was different from mine. It is hard to see if that difference was to do with Rosa being a woman or just being a different person. I guess it was a bit of both.

For Nathan, the key to the success of his working relationship with Rosa was 'respect for each other, a willingness to get on with the work at hand and a recognition of mutual needs'. Overlaying the obvious cultural and gender differences was a recognition that they were sharing the same ministry. 'Having formed a good working relationship [with Rosa], I am convinced that we achieved far, far more working as a team than either of us would have ever achieved by ourselves.' He still wonders what they might have achieved together had Paulo joined the team.

Nathan's experience illustrates an area of collaboration that is still relatively new (or indeed yet to be experienced) in many parts of the Anglican Communion: that between priests of both sexes. The Church now has both a new challenge and an opportunity denied to an exclusively male priesthood: that is, to model Christ's body, the Church, in the working relationships between women and men among the clergy. Women in every Christian denomination are more experienced in receiving ministry from men than men are from women. Women, unlike men, have always needed to exercise their ministry in some degree of co-operation with, or approval from, men. Women are used to working with and for men as equals and superiors, whereas men (including male priests) may have little comparative experience of women. And women are generally thought to be more at home working collaboratively with others. Allan and Barbara Pease, for instance, comment on the effectiveness of 'feminine' value systems that can bring efficiency and harmony to traditional male-dominated hierarchical organizations. 'Feminine values', they argue, 'encourage teamwork, collaboration and interdependence which are better suited to an organization's strategic capabilities and human resources . . . men and women need to understand that each gender system is vital at different times' (2001:279).

Among the many configurations of Christian ministry, it is more likely than ever that priests will be working alongside others of the opposite sex, whether clergy or laypeople. And if men and women are in ministry together, then by definition they form a partnership with a degree of diversity. So the Church can now make use of far greater resources of symbolic meanings, ways of being and knowing, gifts and experience. For priests of both sexes to work effectively together there needs to be some understanding of the gendered differences – whether actual or current in popular belief – in people's ways of behaving and living alongside one another in community.

The God-given relationality that the Church seeks to reflect is revealed to us in Jesus Christ and his community of followers. Jesus modelled inclusive relationality to a point that, in the context of contemporary culture, was shocking, even sometimes to his closest followers. He applied this inclusive approach, among others, to women. He integrated women freely among his friends and disciples in a way that would have been highly unusual at that time. He treated them as subject equally with his male disciples to God's grace. He never discriminated on grounds of gender any more than on grounds of wealth or rank. Female disciples followed Jesus during his ministry and remained with him at the crucifixion (John 19.25–27). He taught women as well as men (Luke 10.39). It was to a woman that the risen Jesus gave the commission to announce 'I have seen the Lord' (John 20.18). His stories included many images that would resonate especially for women – the lost coin, the wedding feast, yeast and bread, the widow. He never patronized, devalued or dismissed women in the way that might have been expected in that society.

As Christians we all share the same mission and purpose, united as children of God in the body of Christ. At the same time, as members of that body, we respect others' distinctness, mindful that we are equal under God but enjoy all forms of difference, from sex and gender to age and race. A lesson we quickly learn when we try to work in co-operation with others is that we all have our own preferred ways of doing things – thinking, solving problems, relating to other members of a group and so on. With difference in mind, we are most effective in ministry when we adopt working styles and practices that respect each contributor's distinct skills, aspirations, experiences and preferred ways of working.

Facts and myths

Research over recent years has looked at sex and gender differences in relationships. There are now many more women in the workplace, in the public sphere, in positions of authority, and so it has become imperative that women and men work co-operatively and effectively together. Brenda summed up her feelings about her preference for a working environment of both women and men, when people are working well together:

> From my experience as a nurse and now as a curate ... I don't think same-gender teams are a good thing – it is good to have the complementarity of gender with the mix of such things as personality, skills etc. Out of choice I would always seek to work in mixed-gender teams.

However, male T-for-G still holds sway in organizational culture, including the way members talk and behave. We speak, for instance, of a police officer who is male simply as a police officer; only when the officer is female do we refer to her sex: she is known as a woman police officer, a WPC. Female GPs are often referred to as lady doctors. I have been called a lady vicar and a female clergyman.

In the past, scientific studies, carried out mostly by men, tended to ignore sex and gender differences: male T-for-G was the norm. But with a growing proportion of women becoming authorities in such spheres as psychology, anthropology and sociology, we have been able to gain greater understanding of the ways in which men and women think and operate and relate to one another, and how they make choices and decisions. Pioneering work by Carol Gilligan in the 1980s and many other researchers since has suggested gendered differences in a great range of human behaviours, from thinking to speaking and working in groups. These of course vary from one culture to another, but will often bear similarities across many cultures.

Tannen reports that where a man and a woman are working together, people tend to address themselves to the man, on the assumption that he is the one with power and she is the helper (1996:114). I recently led a service while some stonemasons were doing repairs to the steeple. After the service, I was standing at the west door talking with an elderly man when one of the masons approached with a query about which door parishioners should use to avoid any accidents from the repair works overhead. The workman addressed his question directly to my male parishioner. Apparently, by dint of his masculinity and despite his advanced age, he must be the one in charge. The mason evidently could not conceive that I might be the one he should consult. Alb, chasuble and stole evidently invested no sartorial sign of authority when worn by a woman.

Other studies reveal gender differences in the way women and men define and use power, how they approach leadership, how they solve problems, relate to one another in groups and learn new skills. Edidah-Mary told me about the Uganda Mothers' Union hosting in 2008 a Provincial Centenary celebration, said by the Archbishop to be the biggest gathering in the history of the Church of Uganda. 'The Archbishop wondered how women were able to organize a day like that one without the males' support, especially in mobilizing the funds.' It is still a topic of debate as to how the MU organizers managed to seat and feed such a multitude of people. However, Edidah-Mary remarked, 'after a day like that one, it is surprising to hear anyone arguing that men are better mobilizers and managers than women – hence the only ones suitable to be church overseers!'

Jane commented that popular generalizations about gender differences at work were affirmed from her own experience. She remarked that most ordained men she has worked with lead in an authoritarian, heavy-handed way, often reinforcing their position as incumbent in debate and discussion:

> They are more structure and role-aware than the women I have worked with and enjoy planning and delineating vision and 'where they are going' as a parish. I remember a friend and colleague commenting once that she finds it so frustrating to work with men in leadership who are trying to tie everything down to a five-year plan because she is more conscious of process and organic growth. She and I are the same age and were ordained together. I told her to just indulge them because in my experience the men can work on the plan and set the systems and checks and balances in place, but as the parish grows and changes and people come and go, process will trump control. In other words use the strengths and preferences of the people with whom you work rather than bash

heads with them all the time. I think feminists would say that this is an example of 'power with' being more effective than 'power over'. I think on the whole, women inhabit power differently.

Tannen's linguistic analyses suggest that on the whole, women try to confirm and support one another and reach consensus in working together, while men typically strive as individuals to achieve and hold on to dominant positions. Other research has found that, in collaborative groups, women tend to value human above financial resources and to move toward shared power, whereas men often focus on positional power, based on rank or title, and they more often follow the rules and regulations of existing power structures, emphasizing financial rather than human resources. Phyllis has found this difference rather disconcerting when ministering alongside male colleagues:

> My own sense of confidence came from my drive and passion to minister and share what God had given me, which seems to me to be an inner connectedness. I also notice when I meet with retired clergy that the men want to talk about the people they know in terms of position, who became a bishop etc., whereas my longing is to share what ministry I have been involved in, and what the people have meant to me. There is a loneliness in this too, I find.

Matlin reports that studies in nonverbal communication patterns suggest that girls and women generally look at conversational partners more than males do; men tend not to sustain prolonged eye contact (2000:205). People are more likely to approach closely to a woman rather than to a man; and two women touch each other more than two men do (2000:202–3). Ros and Jean in New Zealand told me that they both readily 'do hugs'. Jean commented that 'As women we can hug far more freely than the men,' and she evidently sees this as a natural and important element in her ministry: 'We both give and receive hugs, in public, after worship. Some of our parishioners – widows and widowers, say – would never be touched otherwise. People actually come and ask us for their hug after the service.'

Amy, in a neighbouring diocese, recalled how she had been invited to a parish to take a service, and 'just about every parishioner hugged me – I was comfortable with that'. Helen, however, readily admitted that 'I'm not a huggy person.' Her colleague Dorothy pointed out that touching is very much an issue of mutual consent. 'It's a Maori custom to greet with a kiss, and we are all familiar with that at meetings, ceremonial occasions and so on. But for male clergy, hugging can be problematic.' She mentioned a male priest who was in the habit of hugging virtually everyone he met; but she felt that this was pastorally inappropriate, particularly as he was in a position of some power and authority, so that those who felt uncomfortable might have found it difficult to resist his approach. Dorothy and her colleagues felt that the whole business of touching required great sensitivity on the part of the priest.

Nicky, in a parish in Wales, felt that it is much easier for female clerics to offer a hug to parishioners. 'I put my arm around them, give them a cwtch [a hug], even a kiss – it's a comfort thing.' Her colleague, Jack, is more circumspect:

> There is one female parishioner who expects me to give her a little peck on the cheek when we share the peace at the Eucharist. But otherwise I avoid touching – I'm conscious about this as an ex-social worker – because as a man there are sexual implications, and also because it would be complicated with notions of dominance, whether I did it to a man or a woman.

Alice, over her eight years in a parish in South Africa, has encouraged what she calls 'a more "family-oriented" ethos', with children now regarded as an integral part of parish life and worship. A sign of that new ethos is that '"holy hugs" are given and received quite openly and unashamedly by men and women'.

Some researchers have tried to debunk the notion promulgated in popular literature over recent years that women and men are naturally so different from each other that they can barely communicate at all. Best-selling American authors Allan and Barbara Pease, for instance, argue that some women and men 'have brains that are wired so oppositely that the only thing they have in common is that they live on the same planet!' (2001:68). Deborah Cameron's *The Myth of Mars and Venus*

(2007) astutely exposes some of the misunderstandings that have arisen when scientific data have been carried over into the gender polarization of popular urban myth. She warns against an assumption of biological essentialism – the idea that we are 'how we are' because of our genetic makeup, so behaviours and preferences are biologically predetermined, and therefore we can blame any difficulties between the sexes simply on nature.

To take an example: there is a current supposition circulating in western society that women talk more than men. Yet Cameron points out that there is no scientific evidence for this. It is actually a more complicated matter in which environment, culture, social status and other factors play a part (this is true not only of spoken language but of all sorts of behaviours). In a formal situation such as a meeting, those with higher status are likely to talk more; and since the higher status positions are more often taken by men, then they will do more talking. But that generalization is also complicated by the subject under discussion. If the topic is considered a distinctively female area of expertise (say, pregnancy or womanist theory), then the pattern may be reversed. Factors governing the way we interact with each other are many and various. But society abounds in popular beliefs and prejudices about each sex. The danger is that, in acting upon these beliefs, we can sometimes turn myths into self-fulfilling prophecies.

Assumptions can be made about women's time: it's more expendable than men's time, and more interruptible (Tannen 1996:117). Tannen suggests this may be because women are seen as more 'approachable'. I wonder if it is also that, whatever work a woman is doing, it is somehow regarded as less important, less weighty than a man's work. A parishioner once called at my home, and my husband let her in and told her that I was in my office. She looked puzzled for a moment before replying, 'Her office? Why would Ali have an office?' I don't imagine that she would have asked that question about a male priest.

Women clergy may well find that their contribution is welcomed by their congregation as enriching the life of the Church. Ian Jones made a study of female clergy a decade after the first ordinations. In questionnaires and interviews with clergy and laypeople, he found that differences between men and women clergy were seen largely in terms not of innate gender characteristics but of varying life experiences, which lead to different insights and opportunities in ministry (2004:66). Jones noted a growing acceptance of the ministry of women, not least because, in terms of worship, mission and pastoral care, they were seen to provide the sort of ministry that had long been expected of clergy (2004:211).

Gill, who has ministered in Southern Africa and in England, suspects that her sex allows her to be more 'personal' during weddings and baptisms:

> When preparing for these services I have usually spent time with the families casually talking about their relationships and that informs what I say in homilies and during the liturgy. Liturgy is still done with dignity, but with a more warm personal touch. I think I am less likely to preach at people and dispense what might be taken as fatherly advice.

Whether understood as an innate gender trait or as a result of her life experience, Jane (and I suggest many clergywomen) sees herself as bringing a particular feminine quality to priestly ministry; and many who receive that ministry similarly feel that women's ministry has its own qualities which enrich the ministry of the priesthood as a whole.

A Trinitarian model

Dave Wiles is the CEO of Frontier Youth Trust and has been involved in community work for many years. He told me:

> I still come across entrenched views about girls and women; some-times they are more covert, but they are still around. My hope is that Christians will model the kind of gender partnerships that I believe are central to effective Kingdom ministry. We need men and women who will learn from each other. I would particularly like to see more emotionally literate male workers and managers. Perhaps we men need to take some time out to understand what this

looks like and how it might impact our behaviours. This is NOT to assume that emotional literacy is a female characteristic – that would be a huge mistake! I know and work with many men who are emotionally literate. However, I also know many who are not.

I suggest that the kind of gender partnership Dave is looking for – and, indeed, all kinds of good human partnership – can take as its model the interrelationship offered to the Church by the Holy Trinity. There is a wry comment I've heard in clergy circles, that Trinity Sunday is the day for incumbents to invite a visiting preacher to the service or to ask the curate to do the sermon. The reason is that Trinitarian theology can get pretty complicated, and so is difficult to put across from the pulpit in the space of a short address. Besides anything else, there are so many long and weighty adjectives to contend with – consubstantial, indivisible, unoriginate, hypostatic – so perhaps the easier option for a busy vicar is to invite someone else to shoulder the task.

When I was faced with a family service on Trinity Sunday, I took a cue from St Patrick and sent the children out to the churchyard to pick leaves of clover (the Welsh equivalent of Irish shamrock), with its all-important tripartite leaf structure. By the time the youngsters had returned and were handing their leaves round the congregation, I had done the wordy bit. All of us then enjoyed the freshly gathered visual aid, which I'm sure helped us adults as much as the children to get our minds around Trinitarian theology – probably more effectively than anything I had just said in the sermon.

A recent book that has stormed America and other parts of the globe offers an interesting interpretation of the Trinity in the form of a story. William Young's *The Shack* (2008) examines loss, pain and suffering through the voice of a father whose young daughter has been murdered. The protagonist comes face to face with three figures: Elouisa (aka 'papa'), an African-American woman, a young carpenter called Jesus, and an elusive Asian woman named Sarayu. Through these characters Young illustrates some of the themes of classical Trinitarian theology that have been debated and expounded for many hundreds of years. The book has been both applauded as theologically rigorous and lambasted as heretical, with some ministers commending it to their congregations and others denouncing it.

To my mind, the story puts across a very accessible picture of the three persons of the Godhead and their relationship to each other and to us. Like the shamrock, it invites us to use our imaginative and emotional intelligence to engage with spiritual concepts that run deeper than human reason and logic alone. The shamrock and *The Shack* both illustrate something of the nature of the Holy Trinity, existing and working in perfect interrelatedness, harmony and equality. In the early eighth century John of Damascus, building on the work of earlier teachers, wrote about Father, Son and Holy Spirit exemplifying both individuality and mutuality. He used the term 'perichoresis' to describe this interrelational nature of the Trinity. Later theologians have further developed this notion to describe the fellowship of the three persons in the kind of unity that also preserves their separate and distinct character.

This relation of perichoretic fellowship has a bearing on the way we as a Church relate to one another. The Trinity models the values of inclusiveness, interdependence and collaboration among all its members. It reveals an interrelationship of unity in diversity where there is no hierarchy or privilege, no opposition or subordination; each is equally regarded, respected and loved by the others. Although we must not expect to map such a model straight onto our human community, we can nevertheless learn from it in our human relationships. Interrelatedness, an essential nature of the Holy Trinity, is also a characteristic of humankind. From the moment we are conceived we exist in relation – to parents, to other family members, to those we love, to our community.

Modern theologians such as John Zizioulas (an Orthodox Christian) have written about how the relationality expressed in the triune God offers a model for the Church. Being in the image of God, he explains, is fundamentally a way of relationship with God and with creation. The Church, then, 'must herself be an image of the way in which God exists' (1993:15). To take this model seriously means to pay attention to every aspect of community life, from language to worship, mission and pastoral work. It means seeking to end any beliefs and practices that perpetuate invalid discrimination against any particular individual or group – sexism, racism and so on. It means putting an emphasis on interdependence rather than hierarchy, collaboration and mutuality rather than competition and individualism.

We Christians celebrate our interrelatedness with God and with one another every time we gather to celebrate the Eucharist. As theologian Claude Chavasse puts it, 'The joy of Holy Communion is no solitary happiness for any of us; it is the joy of Christ as he embraces the whole Church' (1939:227). The Holy Trinity offers us a divine pattern of interrelatedness and interdependence. We are essentially relational beings, created with the potential to flourish as we gain our own sense of identity and inner freedom. As the perichoretic model of the Holy Trinity reveals, autonomy and connectedness are not mutually exclusive.

We can apply this understanding of unity in diversity to sexual difference. The calling of the priesthood is bound up with our modelling Christ's body, the Church. In this respect, we must pay attention to the way priests work and minister together in interdependence, harmony and mutual respect. In order to flourish, then, we must be sensitive to the great range of ways in which we all understand and experience the complex, gendered dynamics of living and working in community. The Trinitarian model is one that is becoming ever more appropriate to the priesthood as clergy find themselves working not as sole incumbents but with others, in various kinds of team ministry or collaborative practice. They may be part of a group of clergy serving several parishes, or in an ecumenical partnership with other denominations, or ministering alongside youth workers, pastoral assistants, evangelists and so on. Whatever the working pattern, we have to learn to work together, as equal members of Christ's body, so as to co-operate with God in building a Kingdom-shaped Church.

Complementary gifts

Rebecca has worked in England in a clergy team characterized by sensitivity to difference:

> There was a gay male priest, a straight male priest and myself (straight, female). I felt we all deliberately and self-consciously learnt from being in a mixed-gender team. I was openly asked questions like 'How do you experience that as a woman?'
>
> What was really refreshing was the conscious setting aside of any assumption that we all received or interpreted or felt things the same way. I don't mean that it was a kind of 'blunt tool' approach, i.e., you're female therefore you're bound to see it differently. More of a creative questioning of where we were each coming from and what part gender might play in that.

Lucy, a rector in an English diocese, noticed differences in working styles between herself and a male curate:

> In my own experience of working with Andrew I feel that I exhibited an enabling, teamwork-based style of leadership while he found it far harder to delegate or enable than me, leading from the front rather than from behind, which is the style I still feel happiest with, even though I am quite clearly the incumbent here. After he was priested, I think we exercised our priestly ministry in a complementary fashion.

For Lucy, that complementarity was helpful in their joint pastoral work. Both she and Andrew counselled a Christian couple whose marriage was foundering:

> We split up so that he could counsel the husband and I the wife in between sessions when we were all together. We didn't manage to help them save the marriage but we did help them break up in a much less damaging way than might have been.

Lucy asked Andrew to help male parishioners with issues such as addiction to pornography. 'Andrew was able to do what I could never have done myself for those men.'

Joe and his wife Penny ministered together for five years in a Welsh diocese. Joe recalls:

I was the stipendiary incumbent. Penny was a retired cleric with permission to officiate. Our ministry was complementary. There were times when one of us presided and the other assisted and people told us they found this to be a very special experience. Our theology and spirituality are somewhat different yet we worked well together with the occasional need to thrash something out! My strength was in the administration of the parish and in thinking strategically relating to parish reorganization. What fired me up was getting involved in community, for example a regeneration partnership. What fired Penny was the pastoral side and the spiritual growth of the people.

Barry, a chaplain in a male prison, told me of a similar experience in recognizing different pastoral gifts and using them effectively in ministry. Eileen, one of the female chaplains on the team, led relaxation classes for inmates. 'Teaching these men to relax', commented Barry, 'was an important ministry and helped them to cope with psychological and emotional difficulties.' Neither Barry nor, he felt, the other male chaplains would have thought of offering this kind of activity; nor would they have felt competent or at ease in doing it:

> The inmates were comfortable being led by a woman in these exercises – lying on the floor, breathing, relaxing, moving etc. This was a sort of 'touchy-feely' type of activity that the men associated easily with a female chaplain, but they wouldn't have been relaxed about it if the class was led by a man. There would have been associations perhaps with homosexuality, a difficult area for men, especially in a prison environment with a high number of sex offenders.

When Eileen left the chaplaincy, the classes finished. None of the male chaplains, nor the other female chaplain, took it on. Of course, women are not automatically 'hard-wired' to be willing or able to take on this type of activity – this is not an argument for biological essentialism. Nevertheless, both the chaplains and the inmates associated the relaxation class with feminine expertise and leadership. This may be a stereotype, but the fact is that the inmates were comfortable with the woman who was leading the classes, and probably neither the inmates nor the male chaplains would have been comfortable with a male leader. In other words, people associate certain skills and predispositions with one sex or another, and tend to categorize people according to gender. For instance, Mandy Robbins describes female ministers she surveyed as 'more tender-minded' than both the male and female population norms:

> The people among whom the clergywomen minister may tend to perceive them as empathetic and sensitive. These qualities may have a negative impact for the clergywomen who may find it difficult to take tough decisions and to draw a line between their personal life and their ministry. (2008:60)

Conversations I have had bear out Robbins' findings about perceived gender differences. Wade, an American-born priest in Britain, talked about the pastoral care and spiritual direction he had both given and received. Asked whether he had a gender preference himself in whom he goes to see, he responded that he is often more comfortable around women when talking about personal matters. He added, 'Some men are excellent at giving pastoral care, but often men don't do feelings as well.'

We like clear-cut distinctions, and are apt to assume general gendered distinctions where these may in fact be more subtle and individual. Having said this, experience shows that some-times it is more effective in pastoral situations to work with those assumptions. Where both male and female priests are ministering together, then there is more possibility that a great range of pastoral needs and opportunities will be covered.

Jane recalled an occasion when she and her incumbent, Stanley, were anointing and praying for Stanley's wife, who was preparing for a hysterectomy:

> I remember Stanley saying afterwards that during the prayers I placed my hand on the woman's abdomen. He was touched by how natural and easy that gesture was for me (and for his wife to receive it from me) and remarked that in his experience, a man would not have reacted in that way ... stereotypes can allow us to be more effective sometimes and simply more refreshing in ministry most of the time.

Although people are more likely to assume that female clergy are naturally good at certain aspects of pastoral ministry, especially with other women, there are occasions when a male priest is better placed to offer appropriate care. Patrick was acting as a volunteer chaplain to a women's prison. While he was there he was given permission to take a woman, who was being released, to the railway station. On the way, she checked her mobile phone for clients – she worked as a prostitute, she told Patrick, and had a list of over 200 clients. Patrick was determined to see her safely to the train, and accompanied her to the platform where she offered to buy him a coffee:

> I went with her to the café. When the train came in I helped her load her luggage. As we were saying goodbye I put out my hand for a handshake, and she responded by giving me a big hug, which I wasn't expecting. But I think it was because I was the one guy who hadn't wanted anything from her. It was helpful to have someone to relate to who wasn't either an abuser or a client – I was modelling for her a different man, a different way.

As Cameron's work shows, we are inclined to perpetuate urban myths, and adopt generalized presuppositions about the different ways women and men operate and work together. It's easy to assume, for instance, that a woman will be a good listener and a man will more naturally take on a leadership role. There may be a tendency to expect certain qualities in clergy according to their gender, and then judge their effectiveness by how far they display these qualities. Ian Jones questioned clergy and churchgoers about gender roles and characteristics. Respondents who tried to define the innate characteristics of men and women 'almost inevitably reflected popular assumptions about male- and femaleness' (2004:65). Jones also found that a number of respondents put gender differences down to men's and women's different life experiences so that, for instance, women clergy were thought to be better suited to dealing with specifically women's concerns.

Edidah-Mary, President of the Mothers' Union in Uganda, typically ministers largely with and to other women. But she has found a real joy in working together co-operatively with male colleagues:

> I have enjoyed working with male clergy just as one would have brothers in a family, and they are sometimes performing different tasks and at other times they do same tasks like their sisters. Since normally MU is female dominated, we have enjoyed working with Moses and Paul [colleagues in the Mission department] . . . we appreciate their support whenever we have had long journeys to drive or bulky gadgets to handle or operate or even their moral support during MU hectic programmes. We now commonly refer to them as 'Mission Boys' because we have come to very much value their team work with us. We believe the two appreciate working peacefully with us just because we all enjoy Christian team work, where we are eager to complement each other to the glory of God.

Another of Edidah-Mary's stories demonstrates that opportunities for pastoral care arise when people recognize that, whatever our sex, we bear a genuine priestly ministry:

> I was asked by our Cathedral Dean to go and carry out holy matrimony and baptism sacraments in a neighbouring daughter church. After the service, a respectable elderly widower who had just got another woman came to me very excited and told me that although he had outside wedlock got another wife, he had not considered wedding in church as he had not sighted a rightful clergy to wed him and his wife. Therefore he requested me to go back shortly after and wed him and his wife. Ever since that time, I have wedded many respectable couples. I think that after seeing me conduct baptism and preaching afterwards, he believed that some women could perform like men do in church or sometimes better than some men he had been seeing. For after the service he found me outside the church with my husband and other Christians and he sang to me a song that somehow reflected such a view.

Being aware of popular beliefs about innate gender differences in our particular culture allows us to go along with those beliefs where pastorally helpful – or to subvert unhelpful or divisive assumptions. Emmanuelle, for instance, is a priest whose husband is a Reader in her parish: 'His acceptance of my leadership, and our working together as priest and Reader, has challenged previous assumptions and role models of male/female, wife/husband and vicar/laity relationships in the churches where we have ministered.'

What is important in a working relationship is to be aware of preconceptions about gender and to pay attention to how people actually are. Operating together effectively in a team requires each member to honour and to nurture others' distinct ways of being and behaving so as to harness the best in everyone. June told me about her time as local tutor to three ordinands – two men and a woman:

> They had almost textbook differences in learning styles and approaches. The men were both fiercely analytical and articulate and enjoyed nothing more than a good argument. The woman was a poet, artist and dancer, sensitive and sometimes lacking in confidence. What delighted me was to see how, after a bumpy start, this group grew together, with each member learning to affirm and celebrate the others – and to understand the value of their different approaches to ministry. They still meet to support each other, even though their course finished last year.

When Jessica had a male training curate in her parish, parishioners 'loved the complementarity of having clergy of both sexes'. Her positive experience of sharing parish work with a male curate was not echoed in other areas of her ministry. As the first female canon in her diocese, she attended chapter meetings at the cathedral – meetings that had always been exclusively male until her arrival. 'These were run in a very traditional way,' she said, 'no questions, no discussion. I felt there was no point in being there.' Another woman had a similar experience in her ministry. 'Even where men were affirming and kind, it was ingrained in them to "dominate" and do things their way, and they did not seem to be able to encompass true partnership.' Jessica found a refreshing contrast in her

(male) Area Dean's meetings: 'People were free to say what they
wanted, they were run more collaboratively.'

The fullness of Christ

'When I'm gathered at the altar with priests of both sexes, then
together we represent the fullness of Christ.' This was the response of Bishop David of the Highveld, South Africa, when I
asked him what difference he felt in concelebrating the Eucharist
with both female and male clergy. Women and men celebrating
together incorporate the inevitable variety that comes from
different bodies and different sexes, bringing with them a range
of symbolic associations that enrich and enliven the worship
of the whole community.

Jack and Nicky are aware of a sense of completeness when
they lead worship together and share pastoral ministry, for
instance when they have taken a funeral together, or concele-
brated at the Eucharist. 'When we are together, people hear two
voices, see two people,' Nicky said. 'We present the wholeness
of the Church, in a way that neither of us can on our own. In
that sense Jack is not complete without me.' Jack added:

> We can do the wholeness better when we are together; we are
> less whole when we are apart. The notion of the pair is very power-
> ful – it can conceive and produce results – like a couple having
> a baby. So in most situations people will respond and be glad to
> be with the pair – it's appealing, reassuring. It doesn't have to be
> a man and a woman, but this feels more natural, more comfort-
> able for most people.

Nicky consciously tries to achieve a gender balance in services
she takes, by getting men to read lessons or lead intercessions.
Lucy is similarly mindful of gender balance in worship:

> I try to ensure that there are both men and women represented
> up front in as many services as I can, if not alongside me then as
> lesson-readers or lay assistants. This is not particularly easy given
> that I have so many more strong female ministers than male. My
> suspicion is that an 'approachable' male presence up front during

services helps men and boys feel more accepted and engaged even though our churches are really led by women.

Another example of male and female priests collaborating effectively in worship was given to me by Dan, a vicar in a Welsh diocese. He was struck by a eucharistic service he had attended in an Episcopalian church in Virginia when on sabbatical leave:

> The male incumbent welcomed the congregation and prayed for those celebrating anniversaries. A male deacon began the penitential rite. The incumbent preached. The presiding priest was a woman – she donned her chasuble at offertory. All three of the priests moved together into the sanctuary for the ministry of the sacrament. I was impressed at how the incumbent stepped back to let others do their bit – he deaconed for the woman at altar, and she gave the blessing at the end.

Dan was moved by the collaborative way that the three priests led the service together. He had just been appointed to a group of parishes, so the question of appropriate leadership styles was very much on his mind. 'That service said to me that everyone there was equal in ministry. The model shown here was about stepping back and allowing others to fulfil their ministry.' In that service, he felt, liturgy took precedence over leaders. 'It was not so much performing as enabling – something that needed a team approach, with a sharing of roles, rather than one leader dominating.'

Dan also told me of the worship he led jointly with Sophie and another male priest when they were chaplains of nearby schools, and shared Sunday services with a third chaplain:

> We three always stood in the sanctuary together. We took turns preaching and praying. We made a point to be seen together. We even had matching stoles – like a 'team strip' – symbolizing what we hoped to achieve together. We trusted each other, and recognized that each of us brought our own spiritual and pastoral gifts.

The sense of unity in diversity that emanated from chapel services was not lost on those who attended. The headmistress of the girls' school commented to the chaplains that their ministry was the main area of school life where there was genuine collaboration between the two school communities. Sophie told me that she felt greatly affirmed by her two male counterparts in the neighbouring boys' school. 'I'd say they were both in touch with their feminine side, and we all worked very happily and collaboratively together. Temperamentally we got on well. I never had to fight my corner.'

Circles and ladders

Ros and Jean are associate priests in a large parish in New Zealand which has a male vicar. Both women agree that all three of them have a very good relationship, but that their male colleague works in a different way from them. Jean had previously been vicar of a small parish but had no desire to take on a larger parish on her own. 'I'm not interested in empire-building – I prefer to work in a team.' Jean compared different working styles with the three cultural strands (tikanga) of the Anglican Church in Aotearoa, New Zealand and Polynesia. Since 1992, the province has been served by a three-person primacy based on the tikanga system. Jean commented, 'Each strand has its own archbishop and does things in a different way.' She sees this as similar to male and female working patterns. 'We have our own cultural systems here – why should we just inherit the British way? It's the same with men and women together – we need to recognize different ways of working.'

The two women talked of the notion of Jacob's ladder and Sarah's circle as useful models for different working styles. Jacob's ladder in this context is usually seen as a masculine symbol, associated with striving for autonomy and perfection, heading upwards and away from the earth, and emphasizing the transcendent God 'up there' in heaven. In terms of church building and liturgy, think tower, spire, the priest at the high altar, the preacher climbing an elevated pulpit. In terms of people working together, think hierarchical structures, linear 'pecking orders', the boss at the top overseeing others on various rungs below. This model speaks of people being stratified, with the one in authority having various forms of power over others lower down.

Sarah's circle, on the other hand, is usually thought of as a feminine symbol, a non-hierarchical, holistic structure where no one stands 'above' or 'below'. It is a more organic shape (there are no straight lines in nature) so it speaks more of the immanence of God, present in and among us in our interdependent, grounded, bodily lives. In terms of physical worship space, if fits more comfortably inside a circular building. Clifton Roman Catholic Cathedral in Bristol, for instance, was designed around the basic shape of a hexagon, so that the priest could stand behind the high altar and every person in a congregation of up to one thousand could be as close as possible to the altar. Sarah's circle more naturally symbolizes co-operation, informality, intimacy and often smallness of scale – if people are sitting in a circle, the chances are it's a fairly small group, who all have eye contact and can communicate with everyone else present.

The two images are powerful symbols that reflect different aspects of Church and differing working styles. They tend to be associated with gendered preference for particular ways of worshipping and acting. Ros and Jean both felt they were typically feminine in their preference for Sarah's circle, and that this was their natural style of working together. Both women and men, however, may find it worthwhile to enter into the symbolism of the image they associate with the opposite sex. We sometimes need to look upwards, 'straining towards what is ahead' (Phil. 3.13) to climb out of sloth or inertia or to gain a desired goal. We need also to turn to each other, to 'encourage one another and build each other up' (1 Thess. 5.11), to share good neighbourliness and to realize our common vision. The vertical plane of the ladder intersects at many levels with the horizontal plane of the circle; the symbols are not mutually exclusive in what they signify.

The way my various conversations with Ros and Jean turned to matters of personal space and interpersonal relations is in

itself what many would see as a typically feminine emph
Another conversation with Jessica in Wales might also fit ι
category. She talked to me about her role in selecting candida ₋ᴖ
for ordination training, and commented on how she values
what she called people-skills:

> On selection committee, I looked for communication abilities,
> interpersonal skills. These people-skills are so important, being
> able to talk to people in parishes. I think you get things done in
> a parish by starting where they are, where their heart is, not by
> imposing a direction. That's how you get things done.

Some critics have argued that these typically feminine Sarah's
circle-type concerns have caused a feminization of the Church
which is off-putting to men. Where leaders are emphasizing
assumed feminine attributes, the argument goes, there may
be a high degree of emotional intelligence, but the masculine
cutting edge – drive, assertiveness, strength, control – may be
diminished. David Murrow, in his popular book *Why Men Hate
Going to Church* (2005) maintains that the more masculine a
man, the more he will dislike church. Men are attracted to risk,
challenge and adventure, he argues, while feminized churches
offer a safe, nurturing community. Men like to be combative,
women more pastoral. Churches now offer passivity, gentleness
and receptivity rather than boldness and aggression.

Debates about the construction of gender and its impacts
on the Church are as old as the history of Christianity. There
were strict codes in New Testament times about what was considered masculine or feminine in terms of dress, behaviour and
so on. Paul, in his letters, shows concern that new Christians'
behaviour should conform as far as possible to the cultural
norms of the day: women covering their heads, for instance
(1 Cor. 11.6), and not disrupting worship with talking (1 Cor.
14.34). Yet his message was of one who was executed by crucifixion, the Roman method designed to unman and humiliate – a
subversion of the classical notion of strong, patriarchal masculinity. Popular philosophy and generalized assumptions about
gender difference can veer dangerously close to the elephant-trap

of biological essentialism. But what is certainly an ever-present challenge for the Church is to offer a construct both of masculinity and of femininity that is both true to the gospel and attractive to people of both sexes (and of differing sexual orientations) in any given community.

Fruitful partnership

The book of Esther tells the story of a young Jewish woman who, in collaboration with her cousin Mordecai, grows from being an obscure, adopted girl to becoming queen and saviour of her people. Theirs is a tale of transformation and reversal of roles, brought about by the strong partnership and mutual support between a man and his younger female relative.

The young Esther enters the story as a child who is protected and brought up by Mordecai in the Persian city of Susa. When Queen Vashti is deposed for refusing to obey the king, Esther, along with other young women, is taken to the palace of King Ahasuerus, to be part of his harem. Having won his favour, she later becomes his queen. Following her guardian's instructions not to reveal her Jewish heritage, Esther passes on to the king a warning from Mordecai about a plot to kill him. Mordecai then himself becomes implicated in a plot by Haman, who persuades the king to issue an irrevocable pogrom which would exterminate Jewish inhabitants of the kingdom. Mordecai urges a reluctant Esther to intercede with King Ahasuerus on behalf of their people.

Esther now begins to take an active role in her own and her people's destiny. Although queen, she is still in a weak and vulnerable position relative to the unpredictable king. Knowing that the penalty for appearing uninvited before the monarch could be death, she tells Mordecai to gather all the Jews in the city for a three-day fast, in preparation for her appearance before the king. Her plan is not immediately to ask for mercy for the Jews but to invite the king and Haman to dinner in her own territory, the women's quarters. Haman, meanwhile, builds a gallows intended for Mordecai, while the king remembers to reward Mordecai for his warning – on the unsuspecting advice of Haman.

Esther hosts two dinner parties for Ahasuerus and Haman. On the second occasion, revealing her own Jewish identity, she pleads with the king to save her people, pointing out Haman as the wicked enemy. Haman pleads with her for his life, but the king orders his execution and he is hanged on his own gallows. Esther, given Haman's estate, passes it to Mordecai, who becomes Haman's successor. Mordecai writes a letter that allows all Jews to defend themselves against persecution. And Esther writes, as queen and people's heroine, encouraging Jews to keep two days of observance, since then always celebrated as the Feast of Purim.

Mordecai and Esther together provide us with a tale of co-operation and mutual dependence: neither of them could have achieved their goals without the other's help and expertise. Without Mordecai, Esther would not have found herself in the right place at the right time to save the Jewish people. A model of virtue, wisdom and loyalty, bereft of personal ambition, Mordecai begins the rescue effort. But without Esther, he would not have been able to reach the king's ear and to achieve such influence and authority.

With Mordecai's instruction and support, Esther grows from an insignificant youngster into a literate and powerful royal figure who controls the destiny of her people and their enemies. Within the constraints of contemporary culture and custom, she finds her voice and uses her influence to avert a disaster for the Jewish community. She uses her persuasive feminine skills to earn the favour of those with power, and presses her advantage to the good of her people, steering a delicate course through palace protocol and male hubris. Although always in subordination, with Mordecai's aid she wields her life-saving influence by working with her situation rather than by fighting against it. Her partnership with Mordecai empowers her to use her own inner resources to become a force for good, to think, speak and act on her own volition, summoning her experience and skills to her people's advantage. Together, Esther and

Mordecai exemplify a successful working relationship of power-sharing and collaboration between male and female, in which both achieve goals far greater than anything either of them could have achieved alone.

Like Esther and Mordecai, in our time and place we commit to pursue and fulfil God's will. How much more can we then achieve when we work together in harmony, each with our own distinctive ways of knowing, life experiences and skills, yet helping each other to flourish so as to reach our full human potential.

The Ugandan Edidah-Mary ministers in a province which first saw ordained women in 1983. But she readily admits that her country has some way to go in fully embracing sexual equality. She said, 'We have had some number of clergy women working with clergy men in same parishes; and one finds the parishioners happy with rendered services.' She spoke of two parishes with priests of both sexes, where 'services are very vibrant and Christians seem to appreciate the clergy women's services as well'. She concluded:

> To me what is basically important is to know that the Church belongs to God and he has the power to appoint any one he chooses. Therefore, pointing fingers at who is more called and less called is to interfere in affairs that are too much above us. It is more wise to accept each other while appreciating the fact that sexual differences were intended more to better God's work than to ruin it.

5

Flourishing in ministry and spirituality

'He doesn't do gender'

Dan remembers a young girl in his class at their Roman Catholic primary school. As she worked at her sums she began to whistle. The teacher, a nun, was horrified and reprimanded her with the old saying, 'A whistling woman and a crowing hen are neither fit for God nor men.' The sister explained to her bemused pupil that 'A hen can't crow, just like you can't be a priest – and neither must you whistle!' Young Dan was distressed at witnessing this exchange, the first time he had encountered sexual discrimination. Why, he wondered, was his female classmate being denied the chance to do things which he took for granted? (He's now an Anglican vicar, but whether he can whistle I've never discovered.)

While Dan's classmate was being firmly put in her place, the Anglican Church, following the lead of several other denominations, was already dipping its toe into women's ordained ministry. Starting with Li Tim-Oi, ordained in 1944 in Hong Kong, women were later priested in the Episcopal Church of the USA, then in Canada, New Zealand, Kenya, Uganda, South Africa, Australia, Ireland, the Philippines, England, Wales and Japan. At last, priesthood was recognized as a calling by the Holy Spirit based on inner qualities and gifts to be offered regardless of gender. In discerning such a call, the Church was freed from having to dismiss anyone simply because of their sex, and has since admitted thousands of women across the globe. In the Church of England in 2007, for instance, thirteen years after the first women were priested, slightly more women than men were ordained.

Every priest across the Anglican Communion has a unique story to tell about his or her calling, ministry and ongoing spiritual formation within a specific local context. For many clergy, and perhaps especially for women in a pioneering role, there is a sense that time and increasing familiarity are important factors in their becoming accepted and welcomed at a parish level. Where women have already ministered and come to be trusted and valued, then other women find it easier to follow on. The parishes where I currently serve have had a succession of clergywomen. Parishioners are overwhelmingly accepting and supportive, and I sense that I no longer have to play the token role of representing all women clergy. If I mess up, it's simply my own failing, not a signal that women can't do the job. I'm aware, however, that there are still some pockets of resistance and disapproval – not of me personally, but of my sex. This is expressed, for instance, by the occasional individual who will not receive the sacraments from me, or by male priests who will not attend a service at the cathedral if female clergy are celebrating.

The notion of women's priesthood remains divisive for some communities even where there is general acceptance, and this necessarily impacts on the ministry of the priest. When I was first ordained in England as a deacon I served in a parish where I was the first clergywoman in its history. Everyone welcomed me as a deacon but a few could not accept my becoming a priest. On the Sunday morning after I was priested and I entered the church to celebrate my first communion, I found that, as usual, all the vestments and other paraphernalia had been meticulously prepared by the team of servers, but all except one of them had already left the building. This remained the case until I moved to another parish. The servers never spoke to me about this. They were always perfectly polite; but they found that they could not serve me at the altar, and this was a source of sorrow to the rest of the congregation, who were on the whole supportive of female priesthood.

This experience left me saddened but with no lasting regrets about the parish, largely because my incumbent and most parishioners were so supportive and welcoming. But other women have suffered from deeply hurtful incidents during their training. Dan told me of his pre-ordination experience with a fellow student, Vera.

> I did a year before selection in a parish where a lot of parishioners were anti-women but where Vera was already in training. I soon found that the incumbent gave me responsibilities that he didn't give to Vera, although she was a year ahead of me. At one service I was asked to help with the chalice, but she wasn't given a role. It caused massive tensions and damaged her self-confidence.

Ruby told me of a reader who refused to minister alongside a non-stipendiary female priest in the same parish. 'The vicar always drew up the rota so that the reader never had to be at a eucharistic service with her. I'm a good friend of that reader, but if I become a priest, what will happen to that relationship?'

The stories told by Dan and Ruby speak of a systematic disablement sustained by many women in their ministry. Vera's experience in her training parish not only caused a knock to her self-esteem. It also limited her training practice – whereas Dan felt that he was being liberated and allowed to prove himself as a potential priest. In the case of the female priest of Ruby's acquaintance, the ministry of the whole staff team was being constrained by the restricted rota, and the congregation were being deprived of a model of collaborative ministry between men and women, ordained and lay.

Lucy was ordained in England some ten years ago. She felt that for her, the problems of being accepted as a female priest are reducing, but 'from time to time they still pop up, as if lurking just below the surface'. When she first came as rector to a parish the male reader left the church and joined an independent evangelical congregation:

> It was a huge sacrifice for him and his wife, and not a good way for me to begin in the parish. I think he expected I would leave within a few years. A few others of his mindset stayed on, in a kind

of passive-resistance mode, until two years ago when a group left, including them. It was sad and hard when they went, but the work is now much easier, working with people who accept me.

For some people there is a difficulty in seeing priests, particularly female ones, as both religious leaders and sexually active human beings. Sophie, a school chaplain, visited her mother-in-law shortly after she was ordained. The first question her hostess asked her was whether she and her husband were now going to sleep in different bedrooms. The discomfort felt around the sexuality and procreativity of female clergy resonates with the fear of women felt by some opponents of female priests. Elspeth, a pioneer woman priest in Canada, recalled a dean who used to assert, 'We'll never have tits in this chancel.' His derogatory reference to the female body accords with the expressed abhorrence of like-minded people at the prospect of long-haired or pregnant women presiding at the altar (I have written more extensively about this in *A Theology of Women Priests*). Jim Cotter reflects on the diffidence that people feel in reconciling sex with spirituality and holiness. These qualities, he says, must be expressed from the 'within' of the human, the sexual, the earthed: 'To pretend otherwise is to court the danger of the supposedly asexual, "spiritual", ecclesiastical functionary who cannot relax with ordinary humanity and whose voice shows that he has lost touch with his own deeper self and with God' (1992:105).

Where a woman priest knows that she is largely accepted and welcomed, then it becomes easier for her to minister in ways that are appropriate to her as a woman and which may be different from ways that have been developed over the many hundreds of years of an exclusively male priesthood. In honouring sexual difference we acknowledge that women have their own vastly diverse ways of experiencing and responding to the world and to the sacred which are not identical to those of men and which, with an all-male clerical hierarchy, have not always been incorporated into the traditions of the Church. The challenge now is to move on from those kinds of institutional male

T-for-G that left women and female experience overlooked, subordinated or devalued.

Women in charge

When Sophie was a teacher at a private boarding school, the male chaplain, planning to move away, encouraged her to apply for his post. At her interview was a governor who was also a retired priest. Sophie mentioned how well she and the previous chaplain had complemented each other's work, particularly since she could cover certain tasks, such as visiting girls in their rooms, which would not be appropriate for the male chaplain. 'Are you suggesting', retorted the governor, 'that you would want a *male* assistant?' He was scandalized at the implied suggestion that a woman might expect to hold authority over a man. Sophie was not offered the position.

The prospect of women in authority over men has caused a degree of consternation in many church circles, and difficulty for women priests in pursuing their calling. In the Diocese of Melbourne, for instance, there has been growing concern about evangelicals opposing women in leadership roles and complaining about what they have dubbed 'the chickification of the Church'. The effect has been to intimidate many potential female ordinands and to discourage them from seeking selection in a diocese that for decades had supported women priests. Across every province of the Anglican Communion, female clergy have had to negotiate preconceptions about femaleness and leadership in a way that men have not in the culture of male T-for-G. Even where a priesthood of both sexes has been established for some time, women are as yet inevitably in the minority at higher levels of authority.

Jessica, a senior cleric in the church in Wales, comments that she has spent a lot of her ministry being 'the token woman' since she entered the deaconate in 1984. Eleanor found herself in the minority not only as a woman but as the youngest person in a working group addressing the issue of representation of women in her province. To her mind, the men in the group seemed to be operating well beyond their comfort zone, and appeared to be 'quite intimidated' by the subject under discussion. 'They were very cautious about appearing on message. They weren't sure what the expectations were, trying very hard not to say the wrong thing – and ended up being benign but clueless.' The problem of tokenism was picked up by an ecumenical discussion document edited by Gethin Abraham-Williams in 2004. Male T-for-G 'creates a climate in which the woman labours under the burdens of being stereotyped, and her only escape may be as a token woman or male substitute'. The working group concludes that, in a society ostensibly opposed to sexual discrimination, there is 'something scandalous in continuing to afford men such a privileged position in the Church' (2004:91).

Although, at an institutional level, the Anglican model remains far from perfect, individual stories give signs of hope and evidence of change for the better, even in the teeth of some stubborn resistance. Nicky was ordained in Wales after a long career in the business world, and found that, at first, some male priests were less than welcoming:

> I believe this was due to their own insecurities in having to work alongside someone who was a mature woman with a successful career . . . What they wanted was a priest's helper, someone who took 'instruction' and was able to brush up after them, not someone who saw herself as an equal.

Nicky now has a good working relationship with Jack, her male colleague – one based on mutual respect and friendship. Both non-stipendiary priests, they share ministry in a rural parish in Wales where they replaced a retiring vicar. They successfully resolved a potentially difficult question about female leadership:

> There was the question of who would take the title of priest-in-charge – we said we wanted to job-share but we were told one of us had to take the title. We both agreed at the time that Jack would take the title of priest-in-charge for practical purposes, even though I was ordained before him. But at the time we had

someone in the parish who would not have taken to a woman in 'headship' . . . It helped that from day one it was understood that Jack looked after one church and I had responsibility for the other, and neither of us interferes with the other.

They have developed an easy-going working relationship, both readily admitting to their very different personalities. They attribute the success of their partnership largely to a high level of self-awareness, mutual respect and humour. Nicky said:

I can work with Jack because he allows me to be who I am. We're very dissimilar in many ways. He's far more relaxed. If we were both laid-back nothing would happen. If we were both like me things still wouldn't happen – I get worked up about things, get angry. His patience is something I admire even though I can't match it. I am the one of the duo that likes order and doesn't suffer fools gladly so I tell Jack how things are supposed to be done and he takes no notice.

Asked why he felt he had such a good working relationship with Nicky, Jack told me of his previous career in social work. 'All through my career women were above, below and beside me. I'm used to working collaboratively with women as colleagues.' Jack also spoke of the lack of competition between himself and Nicky:

The beauty of being retired and non-stipendiary is that I've no sense of competing – one of the worst aspects of a lot of clergy. As a younger man I might have seen people as rivals, rather than as people. But now I don't have that stress. I enjoy what I do – I'm not seeking greater glory.

Lucy, serving in an English parish, has also negotiated questions of leadership. At one time she was joined by a male training curate. She recalls:

Andrew and I got on very well. He had experienced some of his male peers in his evangelical training course being dismissive of the idea of a female training incumbent, so in coming to my parish he was making a conscious, gentle statement of acceptance of women's ministry.

Lucy has also encountered a colleague unaccepting of her authority in a senior position. Following her successful team-work with Andrew, she was visited by a prospective male curate who decided not to take the position. 'In the letter he wrote he said he had realized that he wanted a male training incumbent.' She subsequently fared better with training a male 'ordained local minister':

> Matt is a keen member of our small men's group, but also very aware of men's needs. He works well with me in an other-wise all female leadership team including our reader, reader-in-training and churchwarden. I think he is able to do this because he is particularly sensitive to what collaborative leader-ship is.

In New Zealand, Meredith recalled an incident with a male colleague that proved to be a healing moment for him:

> I was the first woman priest in one parish. There was a male NSM whom I invited to preside one day while I preached. He was almost in tears – it was the first time that he had been asked to preside in the presence of the parish vicar. I was astounded that he had never before been asked by his vicar to preside.

Amy, also in New Zealand, was ordained while practising in the healthcare field and at a time when her husband was already a vicar. Together they became co-vicars in their parish in the North Island. 'We were totally accepted because people knew me,' she commented. 'He and I did things differently, and this was totally accepted. The parish enjoyed having two priests.'

Alice, a rector in South Africa and the first female priest in her parish, was similarly joined by a new male curate, and encountered not only gender issues but the additional challenges of race and culture:

> He is a 'black' male priest who has come into this very conservative, mainly 'white' parish. He has expressed on countless occasions how good it has been for him as a male to be trained in a parish where his 'boss' is a woman – particularly in view of his very patriarchal cultural background.

Alice's Bishop, David Bannerman, is aware that in his diocese gender, race and culture are all factors that have to be taken into account when considering clergy appointments. He said of Alice:

> She was concerned that in the sanctuary there were all women, priest and servers. She felt it wasn't balanced. So we sent her a black male assistant – he's very involved in labour relations, conflict resolution – and the two are working very well together. He was in a black parish before, so it's a learning experience for him too.

Bishop David is conscious of the need to be pastorally sensitive to the particular local context. He might judge a woman priest to be very good, but in some cases would not appoint her because it would cause too many difficulties for herself and for the congregation. 'You can be so concerned to be prophetic that you overlook the pastoral needs. That way you are setting up for failure.'

In the Diocese of Natal, Jane faced a special challenge when she and her husband were placed together, she as rector and he as curate. The rather unusual situation of Jane being given authority over her husband required a good deal of adjustment for both of them in their parish ministry as well as in their role as parents of young children:

> He and I are quite different in temperament and leadership style so we had a few tense times together in the parish and obviously it spilled over into home. Power and authority were the biggest challenges. Luckily our churchwarden was a man with decades of management and mentoring experience who was able to affirm my role as rector and enable me to maintain a professional identity. We learnt to understand each other in a new way in that year and by the time we left we worked really well together. We would be very happy to work together again.

Looking back on that time, Jane believes that their marriage and their ministries survived and flourished thanks largely to their complementary personalities and working styles. Claire and her husband faced similar challenges of adjustment in their professional and domestic lives. When Claire became a curate

er husband, Martin, gave up work to become a househusband
and more hands-on carer of their two daughters:

> Martin was given the impression by many people that he should
> still be able to work, and not sacrifice his work for what I wanted
> to do . . . it was hard for him to share this with others, as it was
> always as if we had to justify our decision . . . luckily we are a team
> and see this as a team ministry, involving us all to an extent.

Edidah-Mary reported that, in several aspects of ministry in
Uganda, women in her country have been treated as second-
class citizens:

> This is to the extent that even when in secular circles now women
> seem to be more accepted and allowed to share almost equally with
> men, it is still difficult in many dioceses in Uganda . . . I have some-
> times contemplated with pity on the way some men look at us
> women in the church ministry. I wonder whether they ever think
> about how respective individuals happen to find their way into the
> church ministry; are they fully convicted of where, when, how,
> why, and by Whom one is called into the ministry?

For herself, however, Edidah-Mary is thankful that she has successfully taken on important leadership roles:

> There are not many moments when I have felt rejected and out of
> place in the ministry. On many occasions I have felt accepted and
> valued in church – especially in my diocese. Even now when I serve
> as Provincial Mothers' Union President for the Church of Uganda,
> where I have to interact with wide range of male priests (both
> clergy and bishops) I still feel accepted.

Gender justice and calling

A leading figure in British politics, Baroness Shirley Williams,
recalls in her autobiography that 'Like many women of my
generation and of the generation before mine, I thought of
myself as not quite good enough for the very highest positions
in politics' (2009:394). That lack of self-worth, or a paucity of
ambition, is a familiar theme to women, not only in politics
but in many areas of life, including that of the Church. It can

be a stumbling block for women following their chosen career paths, and something of a self-fulfilling prophecy. In a society where male T-for-G is the norm, women are not expected or educated to desire or achieve positions of authority. Girls and women, with few role models, don't think of themselves as potentially capable or willing to take such positions, and don't apply for them; so few women get appointed to the higher levels of authority.

Phyllis became a Christian at the age of fourteen, and through the teaching she received at her church, developed what she calls 'a passionate longing to serve the Lord'. She was greatly inspired by what she heard: 'I longed to give my all to serve.' But it never occurred to her that certain roles might ever be open to her:

> The Anglican Church I belonged to, and dearly loved, taught and demonstrated the idea of headship. Women were strong in testimony and very active within the Church, but it was clear that the teaching roles belonged to men. I don't think anyone ever questioned it.

Many clergywomen today, in contrast to clergymen, don't have a childhood history of being drawn to priesthood, because at that time it was impossible and perhaps beyond imagining for many girls. The teaching Phyllis received from her church certainly restricted her vision of vocation:

> Not only did many members of my church disapprove of women being priested, but in many ways I had been conditioned to be subordinate and therefore not eligible, because of the theological view on headship. Whenever I considered the future and the possibility of priesthood I experienced conflict within.

Girls like Phyllis were taught not to expect to take positions of leadership or authority. Even many years later, as an experienced priest and psychotherapist, she remarked that 'there is a kind of check on my spirit to a degree, which reminds me to "keep my place"'. This and other forms of gendered difference influence and inform a woman's emotional, psychological and spiritual development in ways that are different from men.

During a conference to mark the tenth anniversary of women's priesthood in Wales, Jessica became aware of the hurt many female clergy still carried as a result of their bruising struggle towards ordination. Her response was to initiate an informal support and discussion group for women clergy in her diocese, where there is a significant minority of clergy opposed to female priests. That group still meets a few times each year, with the aim of disseminating and discussing matters of mutual interest, and of providing mutual support and encouragement. Many of its members hope that the need for such a group will disappear as women's priestly ministry becomes more accepted. Currently, however, discussions among the group still tend to focus on gaining acceptance and on prospects for fuller representation at higher levels of authority and decision-making.

I asked the women clergy I met in Napier, New Zealand (where women have been ordained much longer) whether they belonged to such a group. They recalled that in the 1980s women used to meet together with the blessing of their bishop, although, as one recalled, 'some of the male clergy felt uncomfortable about this'. There was a big gathering to mark the tenth anniversary of women's ordination, and another at the twenty-fifth anniversary; but, remarked Dawn, 'we attended this for the fun of it, rather than for any political reason'. Dawn felt it was important that 'the New Zealand church is in sync with the current secular culture and legislation', which upholds gender equality. 'If I thought I was in any way discriminated against I know I could go to the Human Rights Commission.'

At the turn of this century, the United Nations set eight Millennium Development Goals, aimed at eradicating extreme poverty. Among those goals was one to promote gender equality and to empower women. One of its observations was that top-level jobs, to an overwhelming degree, still go to men. Women worldwide now have more access to employment than ever before, but they continue to have less stable employment, to work more hours per week and earn significantly less than men, and to be under-represented in positions of authority and at parliamentary level.

The Church at international level is in accord with the aims of the United Nations. By way of example, the Ecu~ Forum of European Christian Women, active in ove. countries across Europe, develops and supports practical local initiatives on such issues as inter-cultural dialogue, empowerment of women for leadership, and the promotion of women's interests in Church and society. Its aim is to translate the liberating gospel message for women into practical action, respecting differences but naming and challenging barriers where these occur. One concern aired at its 2010 General Assembly, held in Germany (and where I was representing Wales) was the lack of female representation at parliamentary level across Europe. In Sweden and Finland, for instance, women are well represented, whereas in Malta and elsewhere there is a very low proportion of female members of parliament.

The World Council of Churches has initiated programmes to promote gender justice, for instance by challenging sexism and encouraging shared leadership and decision-making so as to affirm women's contribution in churches and communities. But the Anglican Church is itself hardly in the vanguard on this issue. The Anglican Consultative Council (ACC) acknowledged the Millennium Development Goal of equal representation of women at all levels. The Anglican Communion Instruments of Unity, consisting of the core structures of common counsel, including the ACC, comprised 800 decision-makers in 2006, of whom just 30 were women.

Changes are being made, both in the Anglican Communion and in the secular world; but the pace is slow, not least because there are as yet few women in senior positions who are both willing and able to effect institutional reform. Even where women are part of decision-making teams, it is often still the case that their voices are overlooked.

An episcopate of both sexes?

Elspeth was one of the first female priests in Canada, where she ministered for many years and stood for election as bishop before moving to England. She told me about the Canadian system for choosing a bishop. The names of those nominated are gathered, and information about them, their vision and theology, is disseminated to clergy and lay delegates.

> On election day, all delegates to synod meet in the cathedral, the clergy on the left of the altar and lay delegates on the right. The doors are locked and if voting goes on, we are fed at the cathedral till we have a new bishop. There is voting by secret ballot and by Orders. It is a very transparent style compared to England . . . I have voted successfully for three women . . . If a woman wants to be a bishop, all she has to do is get people to vote for her. There is no glass ceiling . . . We have been electing women bishops for half the time we have had women priests. I was nominated for bishop only nine years after the first women were ordained.

Canada followed the USA and New Zealand in initiating an episcopate of both sexes. Barbara Harris, the first female suffragan bishop in the Anglican Communion, was elected in February 1989 in the Diocese of Massachusetts, followed shortly afterwards by Penny Jamieson in Dunedin, the first female diocesan bishop. Australia and Cuba joined the list over the next few years. The consecration of Lydia Mamakwa as Area Bishop of Northern Ontario, Canada in May 2010 brought the total number of women bishops to 28 (Bishop Lydia was also the first First Nation priest to enter the episcopate).

Hong Kong began to debate anti-discrimination legislation in the 1990s. Women's groups started to campaign on behalf of women's rights, leading to the introduction of a Sex Discrimination Ordinance in 1995. In the three dioceses of the Hong Kong Sheng Kung Hui, where there is a significant minority of women priests, all clergy are eligible to be nominated as candidates for the episcopate. Will Newman, a priest in Stanley, said:

> We always remember that the first woman priest in the Anglican Communion, Li Tim Oi, was ordained by the then Bishop of Hong Kong. Four years ago when the Bishop of Hong Kong Island Diocese retired, one of the four candidates was a woman.

To date, however, no women have been elected to the episcopate in Hong Kong. When women were admitted to the diaconate in Africa, no constraint was put on their admission both to the priesthood and to the episcopate. Although there is no legal constraint, however, women have not as yet been consecrated as bishops. In the Highveld, South Africa, Alice notes that 'We do have one female archdeacon, who seems to work very much harder than her male counterparts – a "malaise" which seems to affect us as women as we seek to prove ourselves in a male dominated environment.' In Uganda, Edidah-Mary comments:

> Generally there is no debate going here about women becoming bishops. In principle, they are allowed; but a good number of male clergy seem opposed to it . . . In one Diocese, when they were about to nominate names from which to select a bishop, it so happened that among the proposed names was a female . . . a male Canon stated, 'We would rather have any other Devil but not a woman!' However, some few bishops and other male clergy appear positive about it . . . many laypeople, both males and females, seem eager to see it happen one day.

Esther Mombo, in her contribution to *The Call for Women Bishops*, attributes the lack of female bishops in Africa to socio-cultural rather than theological factors in a continent where patriarchal tribal and colonial factors are still influential. She argues: 'If women are marginalised in the Church like this, how can the Church criticize secular society? Can the world listen to a Church that proclaims justice, human dignity and human rights, while being riddled with sexism and tribalism itself?' (Harris and Shaw 2004:166).

In England, secular culture has moved a long way towards gender equality, and yet the Church of England has, in this respect, lagged behind wider society. Equal opportunities law has an exception permitting sex discrimination where employment is for the purposes of organized religion, in accordance with religious doctrine and conviction. This has allowed parishes to appoint only male incumbents and to retain a male-only episcopate. In England and in Wales, parishes can lawfully refuse the ministry of a female priest, and clergy-women are still barred from becoming bishops. So we have the anomaly of a church that has been ordaining women priests but which does not allow their charisms and authority to be fully recognized and developed.

In 2010 the General Synod of the Church of England finally voted to accept women in the episcopate, despite calls by some for separate dioceses served solely by male bishops and priests. In a compromise measure, provision was made for parishes opposed to women's ordained ministry to have a male priest or male bishop. The province, which currently has four female deans, could see its first woman bishop by 2014. In Wales, a proposal in 2008 for women bishops was narrowly defeated. In both provinces a vociferous minority of clergy and laypeople opposes the ordination of female priests, and regards bishops who ordain women as 'tainted'. Bishop Edwin Barnes, in an interview for BBC radio, commented in July 2010 that the Synod's vote in favour of women bishops was due to its being 'swamped by more and more part-time women clergy', whom he described as 'ladies with time on their hands'. Reactions I have heard to the debate about women and the episcopate seem to encapsulate the range of positions from enthusiastic support to outright hostility.

Even where anti-discrimination legislation exists, and decisions are made by those in authority to encourage fuller participation by women in the life and mission of the Church, male leadership is usually taken to be the norm, and women are not expected or trained to take higher positions of authority. Eleanor commented wryly about a retiring area dean who tried to manoeuvre another man of his choosing into the post: 'It's to do with grumpy old men liking a grumpy old man like themselves.'

Emmanuelle was ordained in England and now ministers in Australia, where there is an episcopate of both sexes and a number of women in positions of authority. Her comments illustrate the value of pioneering women in positions of authority as role models for others:

Knowing there are women who are bishops in the Province assures women, both clergy and laity, that their place in the church has moved from being helpers to male (proper) ministry to being valid in its own right. Seeing other women in the diocese as archdeacons, dean, diocesan advisors, on diocesan committees etc., and having women's ministries held up as examples of good practice, affirms my ministry as equally valid and not second-class or second-rate.

Dan, a parish priest, talking of the Anglican clerical hierarchy, said, 'The higher up the tree the men go, the more alpha male they become, and the less they seem to be real priests – they get involved in all the administration and lose the maternal thing about caring and nurturing.' Is that potential loss of the personal and relational at higher levels of power and responsibility something that women shy away from? Bishop Penny Jamieson (now retired) comments in her book *Living at the Edge* that 'Women tend to stress the servant role of leadership, feeling more at ease with a serving use of their authority than with one of power' (1997:141). Bishop Penny's consecration was for her, unlike her male colleagues, 'beyond the reach of imagination' (1997:1). She found her new role disorientating in terms of her personal sense of identity, since 'women and power do not mix comfortably together' amidst male T-for-G and ownership of the Church, and female invisibility (1997:3, 4).

There are some women in senior positions whose example can be off-putting to other women. These 'Queen Bees', as researchers call them, enjoy being the sole female in a male environment, and feel no need to encourage other women to join them. Claire, a newly ordained priest, felt she had been 'blanked' by a vicar who was effusive in her thanks to a male colleague who occasionally took a service for her, but who only grudgingly accepted Claire's help. 'Do women feel threatened by other women this much?' she wondered. Might a woman put off seeking a senior position herself for fear of a negative reaction from other women, who are perhaps suspicious that she might turn into a Queen Bee?

One negative response encountered by Bishop Penny in her ministry was the bastion of male closed ranks over the issue of clergy sexual abuse. As the bishop, she was the authority figure required to deal with the problem; as a woman, there were special challenges for her in maintaining trust and respect while overcoming the male T-for-G of a 'brotherhood' protecting its own. Jamieson concludes that such issues as gendered abuse of power will only be corrected where men are willing to share their power with women 'It is essential that these issues are dealt with. A church that cannot put an end to its own abuses of power has no place as a critic of power' (1997:124).

Learning grace

Justine Allain Chapman carried out some research in response to the dearth of women in senior positions in the Church of England, where only 30 out of over 300 positions at the level from which bishops are drawn were being held by women. From her perspective in a training institution, she wanted to know what it is about the Church's culture that prevents women from hearing or responding to the call to senior posts and what sustains them in their vocations. In reflecting on her research, she found that differences in faith development and spirituality between men and women played a part. Factors such as a good sense of self and biblical role models of strong women were important.

The subject of spiritual development has been tackled by many writers over the centuries, but that of women in their own right is a new field of research. Anne Wilson Schaef, addressing psychosexual differences between female and male experience, suggests that in the controlling, hierarchical theology of male T-for-G, 'to be born female means to be born innately inferior, damaged, that there is something innately "wrong" with us' (1992:30). This learnt conviction affects the developing faith and spirituality of girls and women, who inevitably find themselves marginalized in the culture of religion, as elsewhere. It presents itself typically in women's lack of a clear sense of self and an overemphasis on dependence and self-sacrifice at the expense of self-worth. There can be a kind of sloth, not in terms of laziness, but of a passive self-abnegation that hinders women from flourishing, so that they fail to grow into the wholeness that God intends. As Schaef points out, 'When we put ourselves in dependent, childlike, or subservient positions, we deprive others (God and men) of the experience of relating to mature adults' (1992:173).

Self-sacrifice can be a particularly challenging concept for many women, not least for female clergy. Priesthood is a sacrificial calling. Henry Balmforth explains that a priest 'offers his work, his ministry, his people, himself on the altar of God' (1963:101). As Christians we respond to the saving action of Christ by offering ourselves to the mercy and will of God. Christian teachers have taught through the centuries that self-aggrandisement is sinful; self-giving for others is good. Many a manly saint has battled against the vice of pride, and aspired, in imitation of Christ, towards total dependence on God, humble obedience and self-emptying service. But traditional teaching on sacrifice and self-denial has largely been interpreted from a masculine point of view.

Girls, familiarized with the ideal of devoted mother and superwoman, are socialized to disregard their own needs for those of others. Stephanie Golden comments that 'it is not some essence of female nature that causes women to be overly self-sacrificing, but rather a basic component of psyche and society' (1998:16). Women tend to dismiss their own feelings and responses in a culture where the sacred and the sinful are identified and named by men. When men teach self-denial, they do not usually mean relinquishing their power over women. Girls, however, learn that self-denial includes serving male privilege – along with the feminine ideal of obedience, passivity and non-assertiveness, and a dependence on others' authority or approval. Sandra Schneiders argues that male teachers 'habitually propose for women a combination of masculine spiritual practice and the ideal of the "eternal feminine" which, in Jungian terms, is more a projection of the male "anima" than a real ideal for women' (1986:38).

Women are warned of the vices of pride, aggression, disobedience to lawful hierarchical authority, homosexuality, lust and so on – vices to which, Schneiders suggests, men are more characteristically prone. Because of their socialization, women's vices are more likely to include 'weak submissiveness, fear, self-hatred, jealousy, timidity, self-absorption, small-mindedness, submersion of personal identity, and manipulation' (1986:39). Dependence, obedience and service are all features more closely allied to the ordinary lives of women, who are largely in subordinate positions, taking on caring roles in the home or outside, and without an equal voice or place in the public sphere. Women trying to be 'good' Christians can be pressured into remaining at home or in supportive roles because to pursue a felt calling to any position of authority or leadership would be 'selfish' or over-ambitious and therefore unfeminine.

This rigidly gendered notion of vocation, together with a learnt tendency among many women towards lack of self-worth and self-confidence, can be especially testing for someone trying to explore her vocation to priesthood, for those responsible for discerning its validity, and for female priests in their continuing ministry. Irene Alexander writes about the journey of grace, accepting our brokenness and forgiving ourselves, as we become aware of the negative effects of our own self-judgement, criticism, shame and desire for others' approval. She comments, 'I have found this to be one of the most difficult things to learn – to protect and nourish my inner being as I would my own child, how to show grace to myself.' But unless we do this, she writes, we 'haven't learned grace at all' (2007:70).

Learning to live freely and joyfully with who we are, in the way Alexander suggests, may impact men and women in somewhat different ways. For instance, women may feel more diffident and perhaps anxious about the unfamiliar prospect of assuming authority. Coming from a history of having their lives defined and ordered by others, a woman may need encouragement in overcoming a lack of self-worth and a learnt helplessness, so as to achieve a healthy degree of self-direction. Penny Jamieson notes that during the selection process women will often stress that they seek ordination in order to serve rather than to seek power (1997:138). This, Jamieson suggests, can be a cover for feelings of worthlessness and also potentially a way of making that power more acceptable to men (1997:141). Joanna, an English priest, recounted:

> My first vicar (passionately committed politically – thinks of himself as prophetic!) had offered me a post partly, I think, because I had engineered a stand against Barclays at theological college. We preached on alternate Sundays; he regularly disconcerted the good churchpeople of the parish by his provocative sermons – and, the following week, I would preach a rather quietistic little homily about prayer. At the time I was (almost) aware of not wanting to compete in 'his' territory; it was a recipe for a quiet life – but I am not proud of it. I suspect I am not alone. We women are good, are we not, at adapting to other people's needs at the expense of our own voice? My own preaching voice took a very long time to develop as a result.

A sense of voicelessness and a fear of conflict in relationship that can silence women like Joanna have been recorded by several researchers. Lin Mikel Brown and Carol Gilligan report finding that men tend to present themselves 'as if they were autonomous or self-governing, free to speak and move as they pleased'. By contrast, women speak of themselves as being in connection with others, and yet experiencing a relational crisis, 'a giving up of voice, and abandonment of self, for the sake of becoming a good woman and having relationships' (1992:2). Some of the issues Brown and Gilligan list as central to women's psychological development include:

> the desire for authentic connection, the experience of disconnection, the difficulties in speaking, the feeling of not being listened to or heard or responded to empathetically, the feeling of not being able to convey or even believe in one's own experience.
>
> (1992:5)

These findings correlate closely with the insights provided by Nicola Slee. She names alienation as a pervasive theme, and a major developmental challenge for women in a culture of male T-for-G. Alienation manifests itself in a cluster of related painful experiences of oneself and one's faith as 'fragmented, disconnected, unreal, paralysed, broken, alienated, abused or even dead' (2004:106). The anguish women feel comes from not fitting inside male-sanctioned models of religious belief and identity. Brenda, with a long career in a caring profession behind her, found that her own sense of personal identity was 'thrown up in the air' through training for ordination. 'I had some sick leave, and this allowed me some time to reflect . . . But I now have a much firmer sense of identity than when I was ordained.'

A feeling of loss of selfhood and authentic spirituality in women is often linked with an absorption or over-identification with a male other. This can cause some women to lose sight of their own desires and wishes. They struggle to name their anguish, and remain voiceless within a culture where their experiences are unrecognized and unnamed. For these women, there is 'a struggle to transform the relationship to the male God such that it no longer legitimate[s] patterns of female passivity, abdication of selfhood or victimization' (Slee 2004:101). Slee observes that the creative ways in which women seek to articulate this alienation, when it is appropriately owned and expressed, offers potential for a 'generating force for transformation' (2004:107).

For some women, a breakthrough of awakening to a new consciousness or spiritual vitality can reconnect them to a sense of their own selfhood and of their connectedness with others and with the divine. Relationality, Slee argues, 'underlies and undergirds the whole of a woman's spiritual journey' (2004:160). For Phyllis, this manifested itself as she developed and practised her God-given gifts in psychotherapy:

This has been a healing journey for me after over twenty years in Christian ministry and it was a lovely gift for the last three years of ministry, albeit in retirement, to be ones in which the combination of priest and psychotherapist were combined . . . I am aware that connectedness is important to me. Belonging is very important to me and I have always preferred to lead from alongside.

Slee suggests that, as women mature in their spirituality, there is a new ability to 'make choices which overcome the passivity of the paralysed self' and a new naming of self, of reality and of God – an awareness that requires new language, terms and images for its expression (2004:134). For some women, this new identity means a rejection of old patterns of religion that have embedded them in passivity, powerlessness and paralysis. Others find that they can move from an experience of religion as an authoritarian set of rules to a spirituality that is a 'personally appropriated process of self-knowledge and awareness' (2004:134).

Spiritual direction

Slee's research suggests that women often experience a kind of 'apophatic' faithing, expressed in negative terms since our existing language and spiritual models are inadequate to describe it. Her findings are a valuable contribution to the growing body of research and experience that recognizes women's faith development and spirituality as having differences from those of men. This has implications for anyone engaged in spiritual direction. Jim Cotter told me he prefers the term 'Godfriend' for his ministry in helping people on their personal spiritual journey. Whatever term is preferred, the guide or director applies their own skills, experience and gifts to help others pay attention to God's active presence in their lives. Gordon Jeff, a spiritual director and educator of many years' standing, commented:

> The spirit of God fills the world, and dwells within each one of us, whether or not we're practising Christians. I'm looking for what gifts God has given each person. Together we see how these gifts can be put into practice. I hopefully intuit, have my antennae out,

with what people are saying, their styles of prayer, the way they are approaching God ... Spiritual companionship is primarily about seeing the potentialities in a particular person and affirming them.

Spiritual directors can be a great source of support through the selection and ordination process (as Gordon was to me) and through a priest's continuing ministry. Gordon commented that one's spirituality 'changes or develops through life, as indeed do images of God, unless there are psychological or other factors which lead a person to get stuck'. He also noted the important influence of personality in spiritual formation.

In addition to the factors of ageing and personality noted by Gordon, there is also the question of gender. Every person is unique, and there is no single female model of spirituality, any more than there is a male one. Joe, a retired vicar, said, 'In spiritual direction it is so important to honour and to be sensitive to each individual's needs and concerns, discerning and hopefully meeting them where they are in their spiritual journey.' Many priests seek a spiritual director for themselves, and also offer guidance to others. With increasing numbers of women joining the ranks of clergy, there will be more opportunity to choose an ordained director of a particular sex. Joe remarked:

> Having had both male and female spiritual directors myself over the last 25 years I would have to say my choice would depend on my needs at that time. I have been to see a woman in times of upheaval or crisis, perhaps hoping for a more sympathetic ear. I would tend to turn to a male cleric for a rather more pragmatic response.

Choosing a director is a very personal matter; it may be based on very subjective and idiosyncratic preferences, but nevertheless, when someone is looking for an ordained guide, sex is now another factor that can be taken into account. As Margaret Guenther points out, 'Both men and women can be sensitive midwives to the soul' (1992:86). Sometimes it is good to share with someone of your own sex; sometimes the 'otherness' of a director of the opposite sex can be helpful. Wade, a priest in Britain, said:

> My expectations of male and female clergy are slightly different. When I go to a director I expect difference. When I appear before a female priest I want her to be the woman I came to for my pastoral needs, not a female behaving like a man.

With an increasing proportion of female clergy, there will be a concomitant need for directors, whether male or female themselves, who are sensitive to the particular spiritual needs of women. Guenther notes that gender distinctions occur in 'language, life experience, experience of God, ways of praying, and ways of sinning' (1992:111). Tanya is an American Roman Catholic laywoman in a caring profession who is embarking on training in spiritual direction. She felt that there may be 'kinds of sins that a penitent woman may not want to disclose to a man' and added:

> I can see all kinds of reasons why a woman may only want to share her pain with another woman, for many of the same reasons that women tend to only share 'labour room' stories of the agonizing protracted hours before giving birth to their first child just with each other. Simply put, most guys 'just don't get it'. I think we really do need to be very sensitive to gender differences in spirituality.

A woman's patterns of sinning, Guenther claims, characteristically stem not from pride (classically seen as the most serious vice) but from self-contempt, a self-hatred 'symbolized by and centred on the body' (1992:128). It can manifest itself in an unhealthy sense of shame and guilt, in passivity and avoidance of anger that can stunt inner growth and repress her nurturing her own gifts and receiving the ministry of others. A diffidence in revealing herself as a strong person can present itself in a woman's hesitancy and indirectness of speech. A woman may benefit from a spiritual guide who can encourage her to trust and honour herself, and to fully value the God-given feminine in herself – her relationality, interdependence, connectedness with others. Similarly, a man may need help in valuing and incorporating the feminine in his own spiritual and psychological makeup.

We all carry with us the weight of many assumptions – some imposed by others, some that we make ourselves – about our inner selves, our personalities, strengths and weaknesses, likes and dislikes. Schaef relates an exercise she has often carried out in workshops, where on a board she draws columns headed 'Male' and 'Female' and asks for the groups to offer terms that describe men and women in relation to each other. She reports that she has always received essentially the same ideas: male is intelligent, powerful, brave, good and strong; female is emotional, weak, fearful, sinful, childlike (1992:169). When she has added columns for 'God' and 'Humankind', inevitably the terms for God equate more closely with those for 'male' (for instance, God as male and powerful) and humankind more closely resembles 'female' (weak, sinful). I've repeated this exercise with a large mixed group of students, with similar results.

There is a challenge here for any director in helping women and men to find their authentic selves as children of God: for men to be liberated from inappropriate expectations of 'masculine' strength and courage, for example, and for women to be liberated from infantilizing attitudes about 'feminine' subordination, obedience, dependency or self-repudiation.

Taboo matters

A particular challenge for women, even in the post-industrial West, is that much of their bodily experience is still not openly talked about (I have written more of this, and its relationship with priesthood, in *A Theology of Women's Priesthood*). Even today there are taboos around physiological functions such as menstruation and childbirth. Elspeth recalled having to cope with a collision of ancient taboos and renewed symbols when she first celebrated at the high altar of a cathedral in Canada. She had been invited by the new dean who was taking over from his 'fiercely misogynistic' predecessor, and who was keen to introduce women priests. 'It was Ash Wednesday and I was menstruating. I was anxiety-laden and guilty and yet rather proud of the fact.'

Claire spoke of her struggles with severe post-natal depression and miscarriages: 'One of the difficult things I have found is that men do not want to talk about these issues, so there is always a hint of hiding your true identity . . . But all of these things make up who I am.' Experiences like these can be highly charged, emotionally and spiritually, and need particularly sensitive attention in the context of spiritual direction.

Women are more likely than men to have to deal with sexual harassment, whether in the form of mild innuendo or physical assault, and conflicting feelings of shame, guilt and anger can arise as a result. Phyllis recalled that, during her theological training, her impulse was to keep her head down, not least 'because I had come from an evangelical mission and because I was a woman'. She became the butt of sexual innuendos from one or two of the male students, which in hindsight she believes should have been challenged. 'My own personal development had not reached the stage where I had the strength to do so, and on several occasions I travelled home from training modules feeling very depressed.'

For survivors of sexual abuse, matters relating to bodies, sex and gender may well intersect with spiritual formation and pastoral care. This is an area with which churches have struggled, and often failed, to listen to victims, to offer appropriate care and to confront the offender. Gurney condemns the type of counselling given to some survivors which has urged them to forgive in order to follow the example of Jesus' suffering. 'Such misuse of both theology and the authority given to promote such arguments needs to be challenged and given serious consideration in the churches' (1997:49).

When Elspeth was first ordained, a young woman came to see her, seeking absolution because she had been raped by a minister:

Since I was still a deacon, I said she must wait till I was priested. She wrote the Archbishop to hurry up and ordain me. She was the first of what seemed like an endless stream of women who came to talk about their experience of sexual abuse or rape by clergy.

In the long course of her ministry, Elspeth has guided many women in similar situations who had never felt able to confide in a male priest. Many survivors keep silent because of a mistaken sense of shame or loyalty. A sensitive guide will help anyone who has suffered abuse to feel safe to name their painful experiences and to express their anger (particularly difficult for women who have been socialized to suppress anger).

Wade's father died when he was only a toddler. He told me, 'I grew up in a very matriarchal environment. I didn't get the whole Father, Son and Holy Spirit thing until I became a father myself.' His experience of loss and absence of a father figure helped him to empathize with a woman he was guiding who had been abused by men:

> I'm happy to give her spiritual direction, and I'm aware of gender issues. Her inherent vulnerabilities as a woman have deeply shaped the way she related to God. She has taken a great risk in coming to a man for direction. She has had to be convinced that she's in a safe place with me. That was a huge step for her.

Slee recommends the creative engagement of the imagination – in art, movement, liturgy, drama – to explore women's spirituality through symbolic forms. These may be especially helpful for women who have survived abuse, since the imagination offers ways of reconnecting with the past and of envisioning a future (2004:177). In spiritual direction, guidance may helpfully be offered about God-talk where, for instance, paternal images in prayer and worship might be painful. Directors can work creatively with Scripture and prayer to offer images and stories that resonate with women, sometimes 'reading between the lines' to find those hidden women's lives, and maybe sometimes honestly sitting with those texts that tell of abuse and injustice against women. There is a place, too, for silences and emptiness as a pathway to truth, and contemplative prayer that leaves behind images and words.

Re-imaging God in female form, so as to affirm the presence of the divine in the female body, may also be very helpful for men, who need as much as women to recognize the feminine face of God and to see the female body as a locus for the divine. Dennis Linn, retreat giver and therapist, remarks that 'None of us can grow any faster than our image of God' (1993:38). To illustrate the point he suggests that if we relate only to a male God, then the growth of our feminine side is arrested. Without both sides of God, we can neither flourish nor come to know God intimately. Similarly, each of us needs to trust both the feminine and the masculine within ourselves and in our image of God.

Discernment is a central theme in Christian spirituality. The process of discernment developed by Ignatius of Loyola, and widely practised today in spiritual direction, focuses on the influence of God's grace in making choices for one's actions. The aim, to paraphrase the prayer of St Richard, is to be free to know God more clearly, love God more dearly and follow God more nearly. Spiritual directors who are sensitive to gendered needs and the different challenges men and women face can help them to greater freedom and self-understanding in areas that can restrict development.

Many women, as we have seen, have suppressed their own gifts and potential because they have been taught that their highest calling is to serve others' (usually men's) needs. They have forgotten the equal importance of caring for and loving themselves – a prerequisite of properly loving their neighbours. Joe remarked that, in his experience, women whom he directs often appear 'less confrontational and aggressive than men. But this observation can also be a perceived as a weakness as they occasionally put themselves through the "wringer".' Wolski Conn gives some suggestions for discernment for women in an essay on the Ignatian rules of discernment. She suggests that the discomfort felt by many women learning to take care of their own interests may not be the pangs of conscience at being selfish, but rather a healthy anger that will lead to a more mature relationship with God (1986:315).

I hate shopping. Privately, I can own that. But advertising media and casual conversations with lovers of 'retail therapy' can make me feel almost as though a gene crucial to my sense of womanhood is missing. Sometimes there may be a need in spiritual direction to affirm those who do not 'fit' the stereotypical characteristics popularly associated with their sex. Gordon Jeff lectures on Myers-Briggs personality types (MBTI), and uses this expertise in spiritual direction. He explained that 40 per cent of women have a preference for 'Thinking' (in Jungian terms), which tends to be thought of (wrongly) as more 'masculine', and 40 per cent of men have a preference for 'Feeling', which tends to be thought of (wrongly) as more 'feminine'. He added:

> This misunderstanding has all too often led to 'T' women being thought of as tough and un-feminine and 'F' men as wimps, but the difference between 'T' and 'F' personality type is a key one in affecting a person's spirituality. There may sometimes be a need to assure women that it's OK to be head-based rather than feeling-based, objective and logical rather than subjective. [In MBTI] the thinking/feeling pair is the only one where there is a difference in proportion between women and men. In other pairs, there is no gender difference, but there is a 10 per cent difference in this pair. Feeling-type people benefit from affirmation for what they ARE, while Thinking-type people benefit from affirmation for what they DO.

The point was brought home to me when Gordon and I met for the first time in about five years. He suggested I may have moved more into the thinking than the feeling part of this pair. Until then, I would happily have put myself in the feeling category, as an MBTI test had indicated many years ago. I found Gordon's suggestion both interesting and challenging, because it indicated that I might usefully realign in some ways my own sense of self – it was something I needed to reflect on and test out.

The wisdom of wonder

'I am my beloved's and my beloved is mine.' So says the young woman in the Song of Songs (or Song of Solomon, as it is also known) (6.3). She and her lover sing of their shared wonder and passion for each other in a beautiful duet of mutual awe and delight. The couple share an abundant outpouring of joy and tenderness as they wait for, encounter and get to know one another, gaze upon each other's bodies, speak together, touch, embrace, kiss. They celebrate a mutual awakening of love and surrender, they know the pain and anxiety of separation, and the happiness of each other's company.

Their relationship is marked by tenderness, and their language by delicacy and restraint. One lover's exclamation of delight is reciprocated by an equally gracious and endearing declaration from the other. Their homeland is an inspirational garden of plenty, filled with fruits and spices, wine and milk, streams and mountains, from which they draw the opulent metaphors of love-talk – she is a rose of Sharon, he an apple tree and a gazelle; her cheeks like the halves of a pomegranate, his like beds of spices.

The Song of Songs is full of surprises, not least because we hear the voice of a woman (the only unmediated female protagonist in Scripture). What's more, she is articulating her love and passion for a man whose response is equally sensuous. Here is a woman who is fully in touch with her body, her passion and sexuality, free to express her desire – and a man who responds with reciprocal respect, openness and wonder. Theirs is a partnership of shared love and commitment, a longing that is fully reciprocated, a mutual passion that is savoured and celebrated. He calls her his dove, his sister, his bride and friend. He is her beloved, her friend, whose voice she longs to hear. They are filled with wonder and admiration as they discover one another's beauty. In their paradise they move gracefully towards the fulfilment of their mutual desire.

Luce Irigaray, the French philosopher, in a short essay entitled 'Wonder', writes:

In order for it [wonder] to affect us, it is necessary and sufficient for it *to surprise*, to be new, *not yet assimilated or disassimilated* [Irigaray's italics] as known. Still awakening our passion, our appetite, our attraction to that which is not yet (en)coded, our curiosity (but perhaps in all senses: sight, smell, hearing, etc.) vis-à-vis that which we have not yet encountered or made ours.   (1993:74–5)

To put it another way, our sense of mutual wonder, if we nurture it, can infuse every encounter we have with another, so long as we are sensitive to the other's unique selfhood, which will always remain particular to the other, however well we know him or her. Wonder, so evident in the exchanges between the lovers in the Song of Songs, cherishes the irreducible difference between the two who love and long for each other. It is precious because it values the partner's otherness, never seeking to appropriate, dominate, silence or assimilate the loved one.

The Song of Songs provides a counterweight to any interpretation of Scripture suggesting that women are essentially inferior or sinful. Here, woman and man are exquisitely balanced in loving interdependence and mutual regard. It surely models for us the God-given, intimate relationship between the sexes for which humans were created. And maybe it also tells us something about the priesthood of both sexes.

Christopher Cocksworth and Rosalind Brown, in *Being a Priest Today*, speak of priestly ministry as longing for 'human beings to live with the vibrancy and joy, trustfulness and confidence, individuality and sociality for which God destined us' (2002:26). Where there is a priesthood of both sexes, how much more thoroughly can it exemplify the priestly calling of all the people of God to love and serve one other, honouring and delighting in each person as a unique and cherished child of God. Where there is a priesthood – and an episcopate – of both sexes, then the Church can validly model a community that acknowledges and honours sexual difference. Such a Church can claim the moral authority to criticize wider culture on issues of gendered misuse of power and sexual inequalities and abuse, problems that face wealthy and developing countries alike, at all levels of society.

To this end, the Church needs priests of both sexes who can minister alongside each other and guide one another in fruitful partnership. No province in the Anglican Communion can yet boast an equally balanced priesthood of both sexes. Male priests can be instrumental in levelling the playing field. Rather than simply tolerating their sisters in Christ, they can openly uphold and encourage them as valid and valued members of the institution, and actively support them in their ministerial and spiritual formation, so that they can confidently take their rightful place in positions of leadership and authority. Those provinces that enable any priest, regardless of gender, to exercise his or her priestly ministry to the full extent of his or her calling are powerfully witnessing to the impartiality and breadth of God's call.

6

Conclusion

As soon as Eve is created, Adam speaks of his delight in discovering God-given human companionship and intimacy:

> Then the man said,
> 'This at last is bone of my bones,
> and flesh of my flesh.'
> (Gen. 2.23)

God declares at the beginning of human existence that women and men are meant to live in productive and creative companionship with one another. But the story for Adam and Eve has no unambiguously happy ending. Their eviction from the Garden of Eden tells of the age-old dysfunctional, unbalanced relationship between the sexes that falls short of the fruitful, mutually nurturing interdependence that God intended. In the fallen world of pain and toil, hostility and loss, humankind is marked by a harmful struggle of misunderstanding and fear, domination and distrust. As children of God we are called to heal the broken bonds between God and humankind, individuals and groups, women and men. As Kingdom-builders, we seek to model the best of human relationships at all levels, from couples to communities and nations, so as to allow all people to flourish in their own unique calling.

In the course of writing this book I have found many good-news stories about a priesthood of both sexes that is paying attention to sexual difference and modelling good relationships between male and female. I've gathered anecdotes from pioneering women who have been nurtured and encouraged in their calling to priesthood, their training and their ongoing ministerial formation. I've heard from staff and ordinands at training colleges who are putting into practice the principle of sensitivity to gendered differences. I've listened to priests who are exploring ways of being an inclusive church in prayer, worship and pastoral care, and are working to heal the failings of male T-for-G that left women marginalized and silenced. I've listened to the experiences of ministry teams who are upholding and honouring diversity in their working patterns, making the most of members' complementary gifts and preferences so that everyone can reach their full God-given potential in taking on roles of responsibility and leadership. These people are 'walking the talk' of their calling, putting into practice the example and teaching of Jesus, carrying his message into action in their local communities across the world. As they worship and work together, they are valuing one another's diverse ways of being, encouraging one another's spiritual and ministerial development and enjoying one another's companionship.

Writing in 1997, Gurney acknowledges that women are 'the backbone of most congregations', but asks whether this situation is likely to remain much longer in the teeth of rampant discrimination (1997:29–30). Since he wrote those words, the Anglican Church has certainly made progress. The stories gathered here tell of how far we have come in the few short years since the inception of a priesthood of both sexes; they also indicate how far we still have to go. Hazel, ministering in Australia, commented, 'I believe the Church is still very much adjusting to women in ordained leadership ... this takes time, because of the systematic patriarchy that still undergirds our society.' A story from a vicar in another Australian diocese exemplifies the reality of this period of adjustment that continues at varying rates across the Anglican Communion. Aware of my research for this book, he tabled the topic of 'A Priesthood of Both Sexes' for discussion at a deanery meeting. He told me afterwards that at least two male clergy absented themselves from the meeting. The subsequent discussion 'nearly went off the rails':

> After a few men had spoken I asked the women, who had been silent, to contribute their views. The first to speak said she was feeling too threatened to say anything but she did pluck up

courage to share her journey of vocation ... There was general discussion that recognized the pain that people felt. We also discussed the positive ministries that people had experienced where there was a mixture of male and female priests ... I think we managed to have a healthy, open discussion that may have increased unity across the deanery.

A church that is truly committed to the interests of all people lives out its commitment in the inclusivity of its leadership. That means doing more than merely acknowledging women's priestly vocation. If it is to enable both men and women to value one another and act effectively together, it must tackle any obstacles to professional ministerial development and to personal flourishing, and promote a pastoral climate that is both supportive to both sexes and conducive to joint ministry.

The stories and comments I have collected from across several provinces and continents suggest that men, as much as women, are in need of liberation from male T-for-G. Real men are liberated into attentiveness to difference, as women are freed from voicelessness; real men surrender historically assumed power and authority, as women achieve self-worth, confidence and expertise; real men have no need to discriminate, exclude, violate, oppress or abuse, as women are welcomed to take their place at the table in shared ministry, leadership and decision-making. Claire, a curate in England, commented:

> When we are comfortable with ourselves, our ministry will blossom ... I am convinced that our [gendered] identity must be visible in our ministry and our differences embraced – we are not to be monochrome, but in glorious technicolour ... allowed to be none other than the person God created us to be.

Priests who are wise to sexual difference are aware of the greater range of symbolic potency borne by a priesthood of both sexes, and understand the potential it brings for spiritual renewal. Alice in South Africa wrote, 'I firmly believe that the ministry of both man and woman is key to the furtherance of God's

Kingdom and Christ's Church – that we complement and need each other.' Priests like Alice can draw on those differences in God-talk in the broadest sense – in prayer, worship and pastoral care – to relate to both women's and men's understanding, but particularly to feminine bodiliness and ways of knowing that have been the forgotten focus for the sacred. In this way they can encourage all people to value women's full and distinct humanity, personhood and potential. So the spiritual life of the whole community becomes all the richer as women and men explore their gendered imagination, experience and understanding in order to respond to the sacred, to each other and to the world. This is doing real theology that transforms a community at the local level of parish worship and pastoral care, working relationships and social responsibility.

On the Feast of Mary Magdalene last year I said morning prayer, as usual, with my vicar. I was deeply touched to hear him thank God for Mary's apostleship, and to pray for the ministry of all female priests. In a diocese where women's ordination is not unequivocally welcomed, it was the first time that I can remember hearing a male priest openly interceding for his ordained sisters during an act of worship. He voiced the support that clergywomen need to hear if they are to be affirmed within their own family. Where men actively uphold their female colleagues – and share their power and authority with them – then the Church can make concrete steps towards reforming the male T-for-G of its culture and structure. And women will be more willing and equipped to develop their ministries fully in the Church. Only then will we have a priesthood that is genuinely of and for all humanity.

Outside a church in Bath, England, is a stone sculpture depicting a basket full of loaves and fishes. The sculptor, Laurence Tindall, carved the stone in its final resting place, inviting passersby to have a go with chisel and hammer (somewhere on its surface is a small chip that was my contribution). Around the edge of the basket Laurence put these words: 'You can do more with Jesus than you can do by yourself.' Our destiny as Christians is to offer all that we have and call our own in the service of God.

When we are able to put ourselves fully at God's disposal – our whole selves, including our sexual and gendered differences – then we find we have done more together than we could possibly have imagined on our own.

Bibliography

Abraham-Williams, Gethin, ed. (2004), *Women, Church and Society in Wales*, Cardiff, Churches Together in Wales.

Adams, Susan (1992), 'Towards Partnership: Race, Gender and the Church in Aoteorea-New Zealand', in Heyward, Carter and Sue Phillips, eds, *Liberating Anglicanism: A Collection of Essays in Memory of William John Wolf*, Lanham, MD, University Press of America, pp. 91–9.

Alexander, Irene (2007), *Dancing With God: Transforming Through Relationship*, London, SPCK.

Allain Chapman, Justine (2008), 'Gender, Spirituality and Power in Ministerial Formation', in Shier-Jones, Angela, ed., *The Making of Ministry*, Peterborough, Epworth, pp. 55–73.

Allain Chapman, Justine (2008), 'Wise as Serpents and Gentle as Doves: Senior Women Clergy Effecting Change by Strategic Working and Resilient Selves', unpublished.

Balmforth, Henry (1963), *Christian Priesthood*, London, SPCK.

Beattie, Tina (2001), *The Last Supper According to Martha and Mary*, London, Burns & Oates.

Berger, Teresa (1999), *Women's Ways of Worship: Gender Analysis and Liturgical History*, Collegeville, MN, The Liturgical Press.

Brittain, Vera (1982), *Chronicle of Youth*, London, Fontana.

Brown, Lin Mikel and Carol Gilligan (1992), *Meeting at the Crossroads: Women's Psychology and Girls' Development*, New York, Ballantine Books.

Cameron, Deborah (2007), *The Myth of Mars and Venus*, Oxford, Oxford University Press.

Chang, Jung (2003), *Wild Swans: Three Daughters of China*, New York, HarperCollins.

Chavasse, Claude (1939), *The Bride of Christ: An Enquiry into the Nuptial Element in Early Christianity*, London, Faber and Faber.

Clark, Peter (1984), 'Snakes and Ladders: Reflections on Hierarchy and the Fall', in Furlong, Monica, ed., *Feminine in the Church*, London, SPCK, pp. 178–94.

Cocksworth, Christopher and Rosalind Brown (2002), *Being a Priest Today*, Norwich, Canterbury Press.

Conn, Joann Wolski (1986), 'Revisioning the Ignatian Rules for Discernment', in Conn, Joann Wolski, ed., *Women's Spirituality: Resources for Christian Development*, Mahwah, NJ, Paulist Press, pp. 312–16.

Conn, Joann Wolski, ed. (1986), *Women's Spirituality: Resources for Christian Development*, Mahwah, NJ, Paulist Press.

Cotter, Jim (1992), *Yes . . . Minister? Patterns of Christian Service*, Sheffield, Cairns Publications.

Despentes, Virginie (2009), *King Kong Theory*, London, Profile Books.

Diekmann, Godfrey (1976), Foreword to Hovda, Robert W., *Strong, Loving and Wise: Presiding in Liturgy*, Collegeville, MN, The Liturgical Press, pp. v–vi.

Dierks, Sheila Durkin (1997), *WomenEucharist*, Boulder, CO, WovenWord Press.

Durber, Susan (2007), *Preaching Like a Woman*, London, SPCK.

Furlong, Monica, ed. (1984), *Feminine in the Church*, London, SPCK.

Gateley, Edwina with Louis Glanzman (2005), *Soul Sisters: Women in Scripture Speak to Women Today*, Maryknoll, NY, Orbis Books.

Golden, Stephanie (1998), *Slaying the Mermaid: Women and the Culture of Sacrifice*, New York: Harmony Books.

Green, Ali (2009), *A Theology of Women's Priesthood*, London, SPCK.

Green, Ali (2010), 'Being and Becoming: How the Woman Presider Enriches Our Sacred Symbols', in Burns, Stephen and Nicola Slee, eds, *Presiding Like a Woman*, London, SPCK, pp. 102–11.

Greenwood, Robin (1994), *Transforming Priesthood: A New Theology of Mission and Ministry*, London, SPCK.

Guenther, Margaret (1992), *Holy Listening: The Art of Spiritual Direction*, London, Darton, Longman and Todd.

Gurney, Robin (1997), *Springs within the Valleys: Reflections on the European Response to the Ecumenical Decade of Churches in Solidarity with Women*, Geneva, Conference of European Churches.

Harris, Harriet A. and Jane Shaw, eds (2004), *The Call for Women Bishops*, London, SPCK.

Hebblethwaite, Margaret (1994), *Six New Gospels: New Testament Women Tell Their Stories*, London, Geoffrey Chapman.

Heyward, Carter and Sue Phillips, eds (1992), *Liberating Anglicanism: A Collection of Essays in Memory of William John Wolf*, Lanham, MD, University Press of America.

Hovda, Robert W. (1976), *Strong, Loving and Wise: Presiding in Liturgy*, Collegeville, MN, The Liturgical Press.

Irigaray, Luce (1993), 'Wonder: A Reading of Descartes, "The Passions of the Soul"', in Irigaray, Luce, *An Ethics of Sexual Difference*, London, The Athlone Press, pp. 74–5.

Jamieson, Penny (1997), *Living at the Edge: Sacrament and Solidarity in Leadership*, London, Mowbray.

Jones, Ian (2004), *Women and the Priesthood: Ten Years On*, London, Church House Publishing.

Lerner, Harriet (1989), *Women in Therapy*, New York, Jason Aronson.

Linn, Dennis, Sheila Fabricant Linn, Matthew Linn and Francisco Miranda (1993), *Good Goats: Healing Our Image of God*, Mahwah, NJ, Paulist Press.

Matlin, Margaret (2000), *The Psychology of Women*, Orlando, FL, Harcourt.

Mombo, Esther (2004), 'Why Women Bishops Are Still on the Waiting List in Africa', in Harris, Harriet A. and Jane Shaw, eds, *The Call for Women Bishops*, London, SPCK, pp. 163–7.

Moore, Geoffrey (2000), *Complete Anglican Hymns Old and New*, Stowmarket, Kevin Mayhew.

Morley, Janet (1988, 1992 and 2005), *All Desires Known*, London, Movement for the Ordination of Women and Women in Theology; second and third editions, London, SPCK.

Murrow, David (2005), *Why Men Hate Going to Church*, Nashville, TN, Thomas Nelson.

Newsom, Carol A. and Sharon H. Ringe, eds (1992; expanded edition 1998), *Women's Bible Commentary*, London, Westminster John Knox Press.

Pease, Alan and Barbara (2001), *Why Men Don't Listen and Women Can't Read Maps*, London, Orion.

Peterson, Eugene E. (2006), *The Message // Remix: The Bible in Contemporary Language*, Colorado Springs, CO, NavPress, 2006.

Robbins, Mandy (2008), *Clergywomen in the Church of England: A Psychological Study*, Lampeter, The Edwin Mellen Press.

Rose, Judith (1996), 'What Difference Is Women's Priesthood Making to the Church of England?' in Wakeman, Hilary, ed., *Women Priests: The First Years*, London, Darton, Longman and Todd, pp. 136–52.

Schaef, Anne Wilson (1992), *Women's Reality: An Emerging Female System in a White Male Society*, New York, HarperSanFrancisco.

Schneiders, Sandra M. (1986), 'The Effects of Women's Experience on Their Spirituality', in Conn, Joann Wolski, ed., *Women's Spirituality: Resources for Christian Development*, Mahwah, NJ, Paulist Press, pp. 31–48.

Shier-Jones, Angela (2008), *The Making of Ministry*, Peterborough, Epworth.

Slee, Nicola (2004), *Women's Faith Development*, Aldershot: Ashgate Publishing.

Slee, Nicola and Stephen Burns, eds (2010), *Presiding Like a Woman*, London, SPCK.

Smith, Elizabeth J. (1999), *Bearing Fruit in Due Season: Feminist Hermeneutics and the Bible in Worship*, Collegeville, MN, The Liturgical Press.

Spender, Dale (1980), *Man Made Language*, London, Pandora.

Tannen, Deborah (1996), *Talking from 9 to 5: Women and Men at Work: Language, Sex and Power*, London, Virago.

The Anglican Church of the Province of New Zealand (1989), *A New Zealand Prayer Book, He Karakia Mihinare o Aotearoa*, London: William Collins.

The Archbishops' Council (2000), *Common Worship: Services and Prayers for the Church of England*, London, Church House Publishing.

Trible, Phyllis (1984), *Texts of Terror: Literary-Feminist Readings of Biblical Narratives*, Philadelphia, Fortress Press.

Wakeman, Hilary, ed. (1996), *Women Priests: The First Years*, London, Darton, Longman and Todd.

Walton, Janet R. (1999), *Feminist Liturgy: A Matter of Justice*, Collegeville, MN, The Liturgical Press.

Williams, Shirley (2009), *Climbing the Bookshelves: The Autobiography of Shirley Williams*, London, Virago.

Wootton, Janet H. (2000), *Introducing a Practical Feminist Theology of Worship*, Sheffield, Sheffield Academic Press.

Young, Iris Marion (2005), 'Throwing Like a Girl', in Young, Iris M., *On Female Body Experience: 'Throwing Like a Girl' and Other Essays*, New York, Oxford University Press.

Young, William Paul (2008), *The Shack*, London, Hodder & Stoughton.

Zizioulas, John D. (1993), *Being As Communion: Studies in Personhood and the Church*, Crestwood, NY, St Vladimir's Seminary Press.

Index